MAGIC AND MYSTERY

POPULAR HISTORY

ALFRED THOMPSON

FV ÉDITIONS

CONTENTS

1. Superstition	1
2. Magic	5
3. Mystery	12
4. Fairies And Devils	18
5. Faith-Healing And Medicine	25
6. Faith-Healing And Medicine—(Continued)	32
7. Theosophy: Ancient And Modern	43
8. Death	54
9. Corpses And Funerals	63
10. Occult Forces: Animal Magnetism, Ether, And Mesmerism	71
11. Astrology And Alchemy	88
12. Spectral Illusions, Ghosts, And Second-Sight	100
13. Theology And The 'Isms'	109
14. Religion And Religions	122

1

SUPERSTITION

General View of Supernaturalism—Founded on Fear and Hope—Present-day Superstition.

Superstition in a nation depends very much upon climate, temperament, religion, and occupation. Notions entertained of supernatural beings or things, though generally based upon one broad feature common to all countries, differ so essentially respecting the form, character, habits, and powers of these beings that they appear to have been drawn from sources widely removed. The advance of knowledge and the truths of evolution have almost convinced us that belief in the supernatural (unrevealed) is nothing but the creation of the human brain, impressed upon the imagination of our ancestors at periods when such impressions were likely to be strong and permanent, and transmitted within the iron- bound certainty of the laws of heredity. Legends have forever been beheld through different prejudices and impressions. They have constantly changed with the media and vistas through which they have been viewed. Hence their different shape, character, and attributes in different countries, and the frequent absence of rational analogy with respect to them even in the same. Where now are the multitudinous creations of the old Greek and

Roman mythologies? Where are their Lares, Demons, Penates, their Fauns, Satyrs, Nymphs, Dryads, Hamadryads, Gods, and Goddesses? And yet the peasantry of the two most enlightened nations of antiquity were so firmly fixed in a belief of their distinct and individual existence that the worship of them formed an essential part of their religions. Who now believes in a Faun or a Dryad? They melted into what they were—nothing—before the lustre of Christian knowledge; but only, alas! to be substituted by newer notions and imagery, purer it may be, but superstitious undoubtedly. Fear and hope are the feelings which make man superstitious. He doubts as to his immortality, his intellect is limited, and his superstition varies in proportion to his preparedness for death. Every truth is abused and perverted by man's moral delinquencies, and the consequence is that an idle fear of ghosts and apparitions and future states is a resultant of the doctrine of our immortality. The old monsters of the mythologies disappeared before reason and religion. It is the question of the hour what will succeed the Christianity which needs reform, or else must be "writ down" a failure.

This is said to be an age of Materialism, and modern science boasts to have exploded old superstitious beliefs. Yet it is curious how constantly old traditions and fancies crop up amid the most prosaic surroundings of modern existence. There are certainly many people at the present day whose belief in invisible agencies is untouched by all the learning of the ages. Educated persons will attend spirit-rapping *seances* and cultivate many small superstitious observances. To spill salt, or to sit down thirteen at table, is considered as objectionable in this enlightened century as it ever was in what we are pleased to describe as the "Dark Ages." The appearance of two or three magpies, hares crossing one's path, the cracking of furniture, the howling of dogs, putting on the left shoe first, the ticking noise of the insect called the death-watch in rotten wood, and a hundred other occurrences, have lost none of the pagan pungency which makes them fit to be believed in. We call our superstitions by different names; but we cling to them still. Matters that admit of no explanation must always puzzle and make anxious. A strange fascination hangs about those subjects upon which no consistent theory has ever been formed

—subjects the nerves and fibres of which have never yet been laid bare by the forceps and the scalpels of microscopic science. It is to a survey of some such subjects that the subsequent chapters of this little work will be devoted.

2

MAGIC

Wonder-working in the Future—Connection of Magic with Government and Religion—The Magi and Mystery-men — Soothsaying and Sorcery — The Chinese "Descending Pencil"—"Black" and "White" Magic —"Odic" "Psychic," and "Occult" Forces—Deception by Art and Science —Acoustics—Hydrostatics—Mechanics— Optics—The "Middleman Theory"—Past and Present Credulity—Spiritualism and Salvationism.

The effects of electricity on the animal system and on the atmosphere have much to answer for in our superstitious observances. Animal magnetism, which is as yet an inchoate subject, contains "the power and potency" of future wonder-working. As among the African and North American tribes at the present day, a great portion of the magic of our forefathers, which was called medicine, lay in working on the fears and imagination of the patients by means of pretended charms and inspirations. Faith-healing beliefs in these times are an illustration, to a large degree, of mediaeval magic. The Arabian school of medicine, which became very eminent while the Saracens were masters of Spain, were well acquainted with vegetable and metallic remedies against diseases. Their knowledge passed on to the chemists, or rather alchemists, of the Dark Ages, whose researches brought to light the great value of the metals in the hands of the physician, and induced absurd attempts to transmute baser minerals to gold, or to find out the panacea for all disorders, or the elixir for the perpetual prolongation of life. The history of magic embraces that of the governments and superstitions of ancient times, of the means by which they maintained their influence, of the assistance which they derived from the arts and sciences, and from knowledge of the powers and phenomena in nature. The tyrants of antiquity usually founded their sovereignty upon supernatural influence, and ruled with the delegated authority of heaven. The prince, the priest, and the sage were leagued in a dark conspiracy to deceive and enslave their species. Man—in ignorance—ever the slave of spiritual despotism, willingly bound himself in chains forged by the gods and unseen powers. Accordingly, the Black Art, which was a comprehensive system of imposture, nurtured upon fear-forces—inasmuch as its professors were supposed to be in league with the devil—was greatly favoured in early ages. An acquaintance with the motions of the heavenly bodies and the variations in the state of the atmosphere enabled its possessor to predict astronomical and meteorological phenomena with a tolerable accuracy. This could not fail to invest him with a divine character. The power of prophesying fire from the heavens could be regarded only as a gift from the deities. Competency in rendering the human body insensible to fire was an irresistible instrument of imposture; and in the combinations of chemistry and the influence of drugs and soporific embrocations on the human frame the ancient magicians found their most available resources. Fables and miracles of former times are a store-house of evidence in regard to the advanced scientific acquirements of the mystery-men. The secret use which was made of discoveries and inventions has prevented many of them from reaching the present time; but, beyond doubt, most branches of knowledge contributed their wonders to the magician's budget.

Magic might be called the science of superstition, or the "philosophy of the unknown," in a sense different from Hartmann's. The Magi, a hereditary caste of Persian priests, first practised it in any systematic form. In the Bible we find soothsaying and sorcery denounced as magic; and the foretelling of the birth of Christ by the Wise Men of the East is a foremost illustration. Now-a-days we find the necromancy of the Greeks— the consultation of ghosts for prophecy—and the Chinese practice of receiving oracles from mediums and from the "descending pencil" imitated by the Spiritualists. Shakespeare introduces *real* magic recipes for the witches' cauldron in "Macbeth;" and the instances of public divination by the Church of England, when general prayer for the victory of British bayonets against savage souls is indulged in, is of no higher order than the superstition of the stranger in the tea-cup, or absolute belief in faith-healing. At first, the priests were the magicians, and the researches of Tylor, as contained in his "Primitive Culture," tend to prove the association of ideas, which accounts for the development of magic, as Fontenelle declares myth developed, in the lowest state of a race's history. When magic became separated from religion, we find the distinction of "Black" and "White." The former was a belief in supernatural powers, such as are now called "odic," "psychic," or "occult," and the latter a sort of tentative forerunner of the truths of science. Egypt, Babylonia, and Assyria brought magic into its pseudo-scientific stage, and extended it to the philosophic and theurgic forms, which are features in the science of the classics and the Jewish theology. "The growing knowledge of science and spiritual arithmetic," says one writer, "was carried so far as to indicate good deities by whole numbers, and evil demons by fractions."

Some of the best deceptions of the sorcerers of old were furnished by the science of acoustics. The imitation of thunder in the subterranean temples indicated the presence of a supernatural agent. The golden virgins, whose ravishing voices resounded through the temple of Delphos; the stone from the river Pactolus, whose trumpet-notes scared the robber from the treasure which it guarded; the speaking head of marble, which uttered its oracular responses at Lesbos; and the vocal statue of Memnon, which began at the break of day to accost the rising sun—were all artifices derived from science and from diligent observation of natural phenomena.

The principles of hydrostatics were equally available in the work of deception. Thus the marvellous fountain which Pliny describes in the island of Andros as discharging wine for seven days and water during the rest of the year; the spring of oil which broke out in Rome to welcome the return of Augustus from the Sicilian wars; the three empty urns which filled themselves with wine at the annual feast of Bacchus in the City of Elis; the glass tomb of Belus, which was full of oil, and which, when once emptied by Xerxes, could not again be filled; the weeping statues and perpetual lamps—these were all obvious effects of the equilibrium and pressure of fluids.

And the skill of the philosophers of antiquity in mechanics is unaccountably demonstrated by the Egyptian obelisks and the huge masses of transported stone raised to great heights in the erection of the temples, which are standing marvels till to day. The powers they employed and the mechanism by which they operated have been studiously concealed. Mechanical arrangements seemed to have formed a large part of their religious impostures. When in some of the infamous mysteries of ancient Rome the unfortunate victims were carried off by the gods, there is reason to believe that they were hurried away by the power of machinery; and when Appollonius, conducted by the Indian sages to the temple of their god, felt the earth rising and falling beneath his feet, like the agitated sea, he was, no doubt, placed upon a moving floor, capable of imitating the heavings of the waves. The rapid descent of those who consulted the oracle in the cave of Trophonius, the moving tripods which Appollonius saw in the temples, the walking statues at Antium and in the temples of Hierapolis, and the wooden pigeon of Archytas, are specimens of the mechanical resources of ancient magic.

But, of all sciences, perhaps optics has been the most fertile in marvellous expedients. The power of bringing the remotest objects within the grasp of the observer, and of swelling into gigantic magnitude the almost invisible bodies of the material world, never fails to inspire with astonishment even those who understood the means by which these prodigies were accomplished. The ancients, indeed, were not acquainted with those combinations of lenses and mirrors which constitute the telescope and the microscope; but they must have been familiar with the properties of glass to form erect and inverted images and objects. There is reason to think that they employed them to effect apparitions of their gods; and in some of the descriptions of the optical displays which hallowed their ancient temples we recognise all the transformations of the modern phantasmagoria.

In the allegorical and mythical tales of the Middle Ages a certain dread personage is always represented as taking a particular delight in cunning arrangement of human affairs. He is variously known as the Devil, Satan, Robin Goodfellow, etc., and he indeed seems to have been thought by some theologians to keep a pretty park well stocked with dead sea fruit for the delectation of travellers proceeding on the high road to that heated realm of his which is called by so different a name. Nor is it among the Christians alone that the intercession of some unseen third party was believed in, for we have traces in Greece, as well as in the East, of a like belief; and the Athenians were particularly suspicious of anything which seemed to betoken especial good luck. Extravagant favours of fortune were regarded as signs of impending mischief, and distrusted, as the gold casket was by the prudent Bassanio. Perhaps the story of the sirens is meant to point a moral of the same sort. However the introduction of this strange middleman be accounted for, the one great fact of all magic (which is not of Divine doing) is that "means" are adopted for its consummation. It would be blasphemy to argue by analogy and contrast mundane magic with that of the Deity; but this "middleman theory "—of which, by the way, the Spaniards have an idea in their popular proverb, "Where the Devil cannot go himself he sends an old woman"—will be shown to exercise as much effect in matters superstitious as it is credited with in the less poetical sphere of "life as she is lived."

To state these facts, however, is one thing; to explain and interpret them is another. It is always found that no science, no creed, has ever been started without the travesty of what was good or bad in it following like a shadow. As the quack follows in the wake of the men of medicine, the trickeries of art in the rear of the true artist, religionism, the mockery of true religion, in that of true Christianity, so the necromancer and the magician follow the track of the men of science. In periods of general scepticism, strangely enough, credulity is very rife. When the educated Greeks laughed at their supposed deities, the fanaticism of the Athenian people was more furious than ever. Magic-mongers had a great time of it at Rome when Jupiter, Mars, and Venus had become a joke. Mesmer and Cagliostro drove a successful trade in France, and they had hundreds of imitators less than a century ago. In England, about the same time, the Cock Lane ghost and Joanna Southcott found believers, not only among the ignorant, but were specially favoured by weak-minded men of intellect. The credulity of the present epoch is notable. Take the Theosophist craze. Here is an ancient Asiatic creed arising out of a special state of civilisation, having a monastery somewhere in the Central East, where magical secrets of nature, long since revealed by the Mahatmas to the faithful, are treasured. Spiritualism is but a more vulgar form of the same delusion, for the Esoteric Buddhist has his spirits too. Then there are the "Thought-Readers." Hundreds hasten to believe in some exceptional power who would lose all interest in it the moment it was traced to some ordinary law. Indeed, such modern magicians are trusted by a class of men and women who are unspeakably scornful of priests and confessors. It would seem that a hankering for the mystical is, among the educated, one of the characteristics of the time; with the mass of people there is no special growth of anything but apathy, if we except a mixture of low religious fanaticism, with a revolt against gin, not wholly devoid of the eroticism to which certain forms of religious excitement so readily lend themselves. But there is here no new form of credulity, nor any attempt to capture the minds of the masses by a pretended possession of occult powers. Salvationists in ecstasy exhibit a very near approach to the follies of the Convulsionnaires. Altogether it would seem that the inherited readiness to believe without evidence, derived from a time when mankind had no recorded evidence about anything, and, consequently, no conception of law in any sense, is perpetually reappearing in unlikely places and periods.

3

MYSTERY

Eleusis and Isis—The Sphinx—Allegory—Anagram and Chronogram—Folklore and Legend—"Fete des Anes "—Miracle Plays—"Church Restorers"—The "Gospel of the Childhood" and "Acta Sanctorum"—Instinct of Mystery—"The Unconscious."

The uncertainty and the mysteriousness of life and of most of its affairs cannot make us wonder at the extraordinary credulity of mankind in matters which, because they are not understood, are described as supernatural or inscrutable. Our ancestors loved mysteries in small and great matters, and even the secret of an enigma had charms for them. The ancient world admired oracles, boasted of the "mysteries" of Eleusis and Isis as the chief glory of these forms of worship, and described the Sphinx as unable to survive the mortification of finding a cleverer riddle-reader than herself. In the Middle Ages architects built habitations with secret stairways and hidden chambers, painters excelled in mysterious allegorical allusions, authors wrapped up their meaning in strange phrases, and the inventors of anagrams and punning devices, conundrums, and all such kindred forms of ingenious trifling, flourished. Even in the matter of a date the ancient builder preferred to introduce it under the form of a chronogram than to carve it in plain Roman or Arabic figures. The same frame of mind which induced our forefathers to believe in the results of ordeals and wagers of battle probably inclined them to the chance of a lucky guess in gambling and taking action in important personal affairs.

In the folk-lore of many nations we have the records of the objective form in which the instinct of "mystery" has impressed them. These legends have grown up with the realities of a people's history and the dogmas of its creed. The Greeks and Romans had their fanciful traditions; the devout Mussulman has a store of lore derived from other sources than the Koran; and the Talmud contains traditions not recorded in the Scriptures. Even less civilised nations overlay their limited stock of ideas with many a legendary addition. But the richest harvests are to be gleaned from the beliefs of mediaeval Christianity. The legends current throughout the Middle Ages are alternately charming, grotesque, ludicrous, profane, sublime, or terrible. An odd contrast of abject devotion and, as appears to modern ideas, strange profanity—of exaggerated reverence and gross irreverence—runs through them. Men believed in the sanctity of a shrine, and approached it only on their knees, save on the day of the "Fete des Anes," when the same devout worshippers introduced an ass into the church, parodied the holiest of their services, sang profane songs, and misused the sacred vessels, all without thought of wrong-doing. Priest and presbyter alike retained a half-belief in the superstition that a knife must not be left upwards for fear of cutting the "angels" who swarmed in the air—" angels " being but a Christianised term for the genie whom the merchant of the East killed with the date-stone he threw away. It has happened more than once to modern "church restorers," in scraping whitewash off anciently-painted walls, to uncover frescoes which would greatly shock modern decency. Yet these had been tolerated by generations of pious devotees. When we read an old "miracle play," with its coarse jests and profane handling of sacred names, we are inclined to marvel. For we learn that only persons of the highest character were selected to be actors in the pageant. And when Adam and Eve were required to walk through the streets naked, the characters were sustained by the most respectable young men and women in the town, who assisted at the "mystery" as they might have done at a religious service. There must have been a strange sanction of "mystery" to account for these things.

Our forefathers devoutly believed that the earth was inhabited by many other beings than the race of Adam. Popular superstition peopled the mines and caves with gnomes, and the forest shades with fairies and goblins, The air, the water, the fire, were all supposed to teem with living creatures. Mankind walked the earth surrounded by a band of spiritual beings. What we moderns describe haltingly as the "forces of nature" were actual, living personalities to our ancestors. It is difficult to account for the origin of these things. Why did they arise in response to the craving of "mystery"? Many are distinct survivals of pagan teaching, the Dryads and Nereides being believed in still under other names. Some of the religious legends are clearly allegories, probably put forth as such originally, and afterwards taken as facts by less poetical imaginations. Some are clear inventions, added as though to fill up blanks in sacred or historical records. As late as the eighteenth century a pious priest re-composed parts of the Old Testament, amplifying descriptions where he deemed it was needed, and inserting imaginary conversations where he fancied the dialogue was meagre. The ancient transcriber of the Gospels or the lives of the saints did much the same thing till the "Gospel of the Childhood" was added to the record of the Evangelists, and the "Acta Sanctorum" became an ever-growing volume. Many a legend may have grown in like manner. But the point of such illustrations is the undoubted fact that they responded to human desires, which, for want of a better name, are termed "mysterious."

It can hardly be doubted that there is an *instinct* of mystery in mankind—partly proceeding from the limited nature of human faculty, partly from our unfathomable ignorance—which inclines the mind to the superstitious, to a sneaking belief in a soul in nature. The poet, the mystic, the spiritualist, the moral idealist, whoever has deeply loved, whoever has greatly suffered, will not hear of a conclusion which forbids the hope of explanation beyond the grave, beyond the confines of human knowledge. Is death the terminus of mind, that wonderful essence, so slowly gathered and distilled throughout countless ages; or can it be that, in regard to mind as to matter, there is a law of conservation which prevents its destruction?

We cannot wonder that the world is still superstitious. We cannot wonder that animism, or the explanation of all natural phenomena by spiritual agency, is as rife now as in the primitive days, when men personified the forces of nature and ascribed the inexplicable to the power of a hidden and indwelling deity. Christianity itself, as Oersted points out, could not destroy that kind of superstition which sought aid from the devil; and even the most materialistic mind still seeks the spiritual in the material, and doubts whether there is not more than a casual connection between superstitious faith and poetry. None can pretend that the strange mystery of birth and the awaking from unconscious to conscious being which has no thought of the future is not the pregnant soil from which everything that is mysterious arises. How and why we are as we are is the metaphysical entanglement which the Pythagorean and Buddhist would unravel by the doctrine of transmigration, the Platonist by the doctrine of pre-existence, Christianity by the belief in one and only one future existence, and most religious systems and philosophies by the suggestion of another existence of some sort. "To die—to sleep—to sleep perchance to dream; aye, there's the rub." This is the climax of human knowledge; this is the rock upon which all certitude is shattered.

For myself, I think that consciousness may vary—from that of the worm to that of the man, from a mere sensation to the inspiration of Jesus, and that there may be states of unconsciousness which are even grander, more desirable, than consciousness. The sweet dream, the absorbing self-hypnotising of the Oriental devotee, or the Nirvana of absent-mindedness, may illustrate in a degree what I intend. With Richter, I cannot think that "of the world will be made a World machine, of God a Force, and of the second world a Coffin." There may be unnameable modes of being—not mere blank non-being, as Schopenhauer holds, nor that Nirvana of the Buddhists which is a mere stripping off of all our present manners of consciousness—sensation, desire, aspiration, thought—as hindrances, not helps, to happiness and peace. I do not mean that the unconscious existence of the stone, of the wave, of the cloud, nor yet the blank nonentity, the sudden precipitation into eternal darkness, and our reduction to nothing, is the only outlook after death. But I do believe that, if existence is to be divided into conscious and unconscious, the division is inaccurate. The word "unconscious" merely expresses the absence of consciousness, while the sphere which is called unconscious may embrace a greater region than the conscious, and may have modes of being among which some greater than consciousness may have a place—something better than the poet's vision of beauty, than the lover's paradise, the enthusiast's rapture, than the sage's peace. This unexplored continent between consciousness and annihilation, which is widely termed "unconscious," contains the roots of what we call religious, superstitious, mysterious, inscrutable.

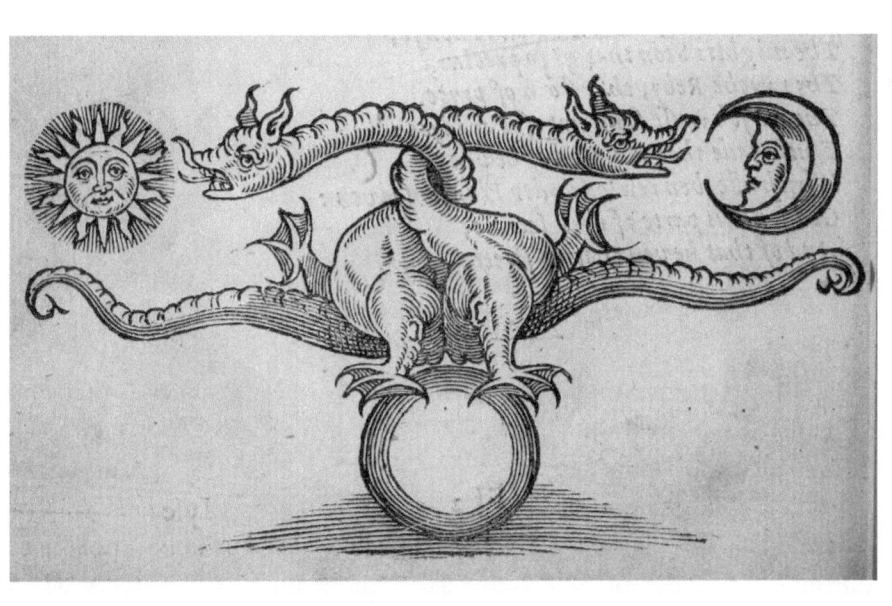

4

FAIRIES AND DEVILS

Fairy Circles and Characteristics—Dwarfs and Malignant Spirits — Origin—Invisibility—Elf Arrows— "The Changeling" — Banshee— Keening— Wake — Mermen—The Medium of the Unseen.

It is rather a melancholy truth that the world is getting prosier and duller as it grows older. "It was never a merry world," says Sheldon, "since the fairies left off dancing." Alas! it is not that the fairies have left off dancing, but that the world's united wisdom has become too dull to perceive them. Fairy revels on yellow sands or in the moonlit glades of woods are as frequent now as they were when Oberon and Titania quarrelled and Puck made an ass of Bottom the Weaver in the woods of Athens. But foolish to us seem those old-fashioned folk who readily imagined that the sylvan and floral world was peopled with gay intelligences, and easily attached to every flower some spiritual significance, some poetic fancy, or the embodiment of some religious legend or tradition. No longer do we peep into the dainty bells of the wild fox-glove, and recognise there the hiding places of the fairies, nor can we fancy that mushroom rings in grass lands are fairy circles, where delicate creatures with gauzy wings tripped the light fantastic toe while mortals slept. School Boards and scientific primers have tolled the knell of such conceits.

There is one characteristic which appears to distinguish the fairy from every other being of a similar order. Most spirits could contract their bulk at will; the fairy alone was regarded as essentially small in size. Dwarfs, brownies, and the like are represented as deformed creatures; but the fairy is usually a beautiful miniature of the human being, perfect in face and form. The origin of the fairy superstition is ascribed by most writers to the Celtic people. But the Gothic tribes introduced the evil attributes, such as the elfin and dwarfish malignancy of the northern spirits, with those proper to fairies. In Scotland the fairies were called the Good Neighbours, or Men of Peace; the bad spirits were devoted to the kidnapping of human beings, especially unchristened children; and in Ireland to this day, when a young woman falls a victim to puerperal disease, the more ignorant of the country people believe that she has been abducted to be a nurse to the fairies. The fairies are always represented as living, like mankind, in societies, and under a monarchical form of government. The Salic law did not prevail; for we hear more often of fairy queens than fairy kings. Their kingdom was somewhere underground. The origin of fairies is buried in a mythological mist. It is said that, during the war of Lucifer in heaven, the angels were divided into three classes. The first were the supporters of the Omnipotent, the second the henchmen of the great apostate, and the third consisted of those who refused to serve either power. This latter class, says the tradition, were hurled out of heaven to wind and water, where they are to remain ignorant of their fate until the day of judgment. This little fable is somewhat older than that of the "fall of man." From a very early period every fairy annalist concurred in giving to the King and Queen of the fairies the names of Oberon and Titania. Oberon was the Elbrich or Rich Elf of the Germans, and was endowed with his mediaeval name by the old French romancers, who represented him as a tiny creature of great beauty, with a crown of jewels on his head, and a horn in his hand that set all who heard it dancing. The power which fairies had in making themselves invisible enabled them to perform all sorts of odd antics. German sprites—those dishonest little beings who are addicted to stealing the farmers' crops of peas—are generally furnished with a magic cap when they are bent on their mischievous errands. One of the elfin princesses in Andersen's stories has the convenient power of vanishing by putting a wand in her mouth. In the same way Shakespeare— pre-eminent poet on the subject, whose Queen Mab has almost dethroned Titania—attributes to his fairies this faculty of rendering themselves invisible. Oberon in "A Midsummer Night's Dream," and Prospero in "The Tempest," declare their power of becoming invisible. Indeed, in most of the fairy legends and folk tales we find this superhuman quality of disappearing at will amply illustrated. Many a German peasant now-a-days will not frequent certain localities for fear of falling under the irresistible influence of these unseen beings. In some parts of the continent, when a strong hurricane rages, the phenomenon is regarded by many as nothing less than one of the chief fairies making her invisible circuit. When the wind howls loudly in West Flanders the people say: "Hark, Alvina weeps"—Alvina being the daughter of a king who, on account of her marriage, was cursed by her parents to wander about forever, like the fairies, invisible.

The evil spirits occupy a weird and awful place in tradition. Every one has heard of the "elf arrows those fairy weapons of myth, shot mostly destructively, which probably are a survival of the Stone Age. Not content with the advantage of waging war in an invisible armour, and the spiritual power of neolithic arrowheads, the evil creatures stole, as I have said, children; and in Scotland various charms were used for their restoration. The most efficacious was believed to be the roasting of the supposititious child or "changeling" which the fairies had left in place of the infant kidnapped. It was understood that the false babe would disappear and the true one be left in its place. Possession of what are called toad-stones was also held to be an efficient preservative against the abduction of children by the fairies. The introduction of the Banshee in the following stanza of a "Keening"— an Irish term for a wild song of lamentation poured forth over a dead body in the course of the "wake" ceremony by certain mourners employed for the purpose—indicates the popular feeling on the subject:—

> " 'Twas the Banshee's lonely wailing,
> Well I knew the voice of death
> In the night wind slowly sailing

O'er the bleak and gloomy heath."

This Banshee was a mysterious personage, generally supposed to be the harbinger of some approaching misfortune. The superstition was not confined to Ireland, for several families of the Highlands of Scotland formerly laid claim to the distinction of an attendant spirit, who performed the office of the Irish Banshee—an office which honoured the decease, according to Sir Walter Scott, of members of those families only which were of pure Milesian blood. Welsh clans also have another form of the Banshee in the "Cyhyraeth," which is never seen, although the noise it makes is such as to inspire fear in those who hear it. As an instance, too, of how superstitions travel from one country to another, we are told that, in America, there are tales of the Banshee imported from Ireland along with the sons of that soil.

Numberless stories of a ridiculous kind have been related concerning the intercourse of the fairies with mankind. Some of the poor creatures arraigned in past times for witchcraft admitted, under torture, having had correspondence with fairies. The trials of Bessie Dunlop and Alison Pearson, in the years 1576 and 1588, in Scotland, illustrate this statement. But the unfortunate creatures who confessed their intercouse with fairyland could not so save themselves. They were convicted and burned at the stake. It can hardly be doubted that these animistic beings have had some common source, and that martyrdom was often a result of sincere belief in their existence. In a primitive condition of the world's races human energy found an outlet in imagination, and the vagaries of which this faculty is capable are unlimited. The belief that men's souls left their bodies at death to float about the air until they found some other habitat into which they could transmigrate, readily adapted itself to an objective explanation. Traces of fairy lore may be detected in the populous pantheons of antiquity, in the Fates of the Romans who presided at birth and influenced destiny, the Peri of the Persians, the malignant Jays of the Middle Ages, and the Pluto and Proserpine dynasty which Chaucer mentions. In the "Eddas," the elves and hobgoblins are represented as dwelling in the clay, much as worms located themselves in the human flesh. Plutarch points out the almost immemorial prevalence of belief in two principles—one the author of good, and the other the author of bad. Of course it was easy enough to engraft upon each of these the ideas of supporting spirits for and against, the hosts being generalled on the one side by the Good Power, on the other by the Bad, who became known later as the Devil. Christianity merely changed the way of regarding these creatures; but I shall relegate detailed consideration of this phase of the subject to another chapter, where demonology will receive due treatment.

These superstitions are far from extinct in the British Islands. It is little over a hundred years ago that the belief in supernatural "middlemen" was common among all classes. To-day the belief is little diminished. The gloomy and fanatic religion of Scotland is not the only system of the after-life which is responsible for the faith in the personal appearance of devils. Those mean pranks of Satan in assaulting ministers, waylaying travellers, and disturbing families while at worship, are but illustrative of the same instinct which induced the phantasy of fairy beings. It was not only in air and on land that the invisibles exercised their sway. Mermen and mermaids—those sirens of the ocean who were supposed to be such terrors to over-confiding navigators—and the water imps and witches, have occupied a large place among the stories of the river and sea demons. The Rosicrucians, called by a play upon the name of the founder, followers of the Rosy Cross, are a comparatively recent body of believers, who are largely responsible for Theosophy and similar fancies, which are but a modernised reflection of what they taught. More graceful than demonology, the philosophy of Rosencreutz has found annotation in the Sylphs, Ariels, and Sylphids of Shakespeare and other English poets, and has furnished conceits for Fouque's "Undine," Bulwer's "Zanoni," Dr. Mackay's "Salamandrine," and other literary mooning. It was a curious and charming creed that the elements swarmed not with ghouls, but with angels, more ready to be kind than cruel. Given an earth inhabited by Gnomes, the air by Sylphs, the fire by Salamanders, and the water by Nymphs or Undines, and the mystic mind can easily conclude that the elixir of life, the philosopher's stone, essence of invisibility, the secret of omnipotence, and perpetual motion are all within grasp. But in this, as in most systems, the "middle-man" difficulty again appears. Communication with the unseen powers should make the problems of philosophy no longer a puzzle. But there is something wrong with the medium.

It is easy to conclude that more than ignorance is responsible for these superstitions. True, when the human mind allows itself to dwell upon and worry over ordinary matters as things taking place by invisible agents, such as spirits, demons, apparitions, charms, there is no limiting the powers they are supposed to perform. But ignorance is not alone responsible for this peculiar mental or emotional or hereditary weakness.

5

FAITH-HEALING AND MEDICINE

Supernatural Sources of Disease—Witchcraft and Spells —Occult Cures— Charms and Love Philtres—The Royal Touch—Demon, Ghost, and Animal Souls— Totemism—Exorcising the "Possessed"—Paracelsus— "The Doctrine of Signatures"—Botanical Medicine —The Colour Cure—Music and Medicine— Electro- Therapeutics—"Devil-Dances."

Sir Charles Bell declared that human sufferings and human credulity afford a never-failing harvest; for quackery is an evil—

" Which walks unchecked and triumphs in the sun."

The popular belief in olden days was that, as diseases were produced by supernatural power, so they were to be cured by it. In "The History of European Civilisation" it is pointed out that barbarous people always ascribe to their good or evil deities not only extraordinary diseases, but many of the ordinary diseases to which humanity is liable. Throughout Europe the idea of disease as of supernatural origin long retained its hold, and, in our own country, such a notion naturally encouraged all kinds of quackery. The great witchcraft movement afforded abundant opportunities for its agents to practise their spells, survivals of which linger on in many a country village. Credulity in former centuries as to matters of "curing" is evidenced by the Act of Henry VIII., specially passed to protect "wise women" and others who were supposed to heal by their magic arts—such persons being described as "endued by God with the knowledge of herbs, roots, and waters.

Accordingly, anyone who gathered herbs and professed to remove disease by occult means was submitted to with unquestioning faith. Thus, tumours, on their advice, were supposed to be removed by stroking them with the hand of a dead man, and chips of a hangman's tree or scaffold worn as amulets were reckoned a most efficacious remedy against ague. These mediaeval quacks were more or less supported by the learned of their day. The man of science was generally somewhat of an alchemist, and the students of medicine were usually extensive dealers in charms and philtres. The apothecary himself was as ready to sell love-philtres to a maiden as narcotics to a friar. Lord Bacon laid it down as credible that precious stones could cure maladies, and Sir Thomas Browne believed in witchcraft to the same end. In 1553 Cecil, the ancestor of Lord Salisbury, is recommended by Lord Audley to place reliance in the healing virtues of a "sow pig nine days old," distilled with various herbs and spices; and as late as 1829 Mr. Forster, infected with the same spirit, wrote a book to prove that epidemics are due to the shocks of clashing comets. Many persons of position submitted to the ceremony of healing by the royal touch, and it is recorded that Charles II. touched about 92,000 persons. William III. regarded the practice as foolish, and upon the only occasion he laid his hand on a patient he said: "God give you better health—*and more sense.*"

It is needful to consider the condition of primitive man before any clear conception in regard to the mythical bearing of the art of medicine can be arrived at. We find that the earliest religions included the idea of demons, which are but spirits of a more or less modified soul, whether of an animal or a human being, a stick or stone. The savage saw that the difference between the living body and the dead was—breath. Hence the breath which left the dying man was his life, and his life or soul went into the atmosphere, where it still lived, in the form of a spirit or demon—a notion upon which the modern

Spiritualist has made little improvement. In their dreams and disordered nervous states the pre-historic people saw visions which, if they had possessed the spectroscope, they would have known were not ghost-souls. Thus, in cases of disease among races of low culture the morbid state of the body and mind (notable in persons suffering from *delirium tremens*) of the patient led him to conclude that he was "possessed" with an evil spirit. Then his friends, to appease the wrath of the demon, made sacrifices—much as the good Catholic pays his priest to have his friend's soul released from purgatory—and resorted to exorcism or charms and incantations, designed to drive away the unseen evil thing. This is one phase of Totemism, or the primitive belief in a guardian demon, whether animal, vegetable, or mineral, common to all the early communities. Not only, as I have said, had human beings souls, but the animals, the plants, inanimate things, the stars, the earth, the thunder, sun, moon, sky, all had souls. It was natural then for the savage to worship and sacrifice to these Nature-Souls, whom he feared and could not over-awe. His only idea of force was force in his own shape, though invisible. Accordingly, he imagined deities—superior powers—corresponding to different types of men—anthropomorphism. It was observed that the rising of the stars was analogous to the phenomenon of birth; and this, with other analogies, led to the fancied relation between the heavenly bodies and the human frame. Centuries after, alchemy is found engaged in seeking this correspondence between the metals and the planets—the star Mercury and the chemical mercury, for example—and astrology lends its aid in the cosmical search for the elixir of life and the secret of perpetual rejuvenescence. Paracelsus, in the Middle Ages, systematised these beliefs, and explained that the human body was a "microcosm," which corresponded to the "macrocosm," and contained in itself all parts of visible nature—sun, moon, stars, and the poles of heaven. Accordingly, it was for the physician to study external nature, because diseases were not natural, but spiritual.

In this way arose the famous "Doctrine of Signatures," or the proposal that signs indicate the virtues and uses of natural objects. This doctrine was one of the most popular theories of bygone times, and crystallised, through the aid of Bohme, the early faith in "sympathy," which I shall show to be the lineal predecessor of what are known to-day as hypnotism, spirit cures, electrobiology, and the like. According to its teaching, it was thought that objects, by their external character, indicated the particular diseases for which nature had intended them as remedies. Thus it was asserted that the properties of substances were often denoted by their colour: white was regarded as cooling, and red as hot. For disorders of the blood burnt purple, pomegranates, mulberries, and other red ingredients were dissolved in the patient's drink; and for liver complaints yellow substances were recommended. Pliny spoke of the folly of magicians in using catanance for love-potions, though the practice prevailed for centuries after. Coles, in his "Art of Simpling" (1656), tells us how God has imprinted on herbs a distinct form, and given them particular signs or signatures by which man can read the use of them. The malignant plants, for instance, showed their nature by the sad and melancholic appearance of their leaves, flowers, or fruit. Euphrasia, or eye-bright, was supposed to be good for the eye, owing to a black pupil-like spot in its corolla. Milton represents the Archangel clearing the vision of Adam and Eve by its means, and Spenser speaks of it in the same strain. The ginseng was said by the Chinese and American Indians to possess virtues deduced from the root which resembles the human body. The Romans had their rock-breaking plant called "Saxifraga," which was considered efficacious in the cure of callulous complaints; and hence the popular name, stone-breaking. It was once believed that the seeds of ferns could produce invisibility, and Shakespeare makes Gadshill speak of it in "Henry IV." The walnut was considered good for mental diseases from its representing the structure of the human head. Our Lady's Thistle, from its many prickles, was recommended for stitches in the side; and nettle-tea is still popular in cases of nettle-rash. The berberry tree and turmeric—both yellow plants— were recommended for jaundice; for ague there was quaking grass; and as the cones of the pine tree resemble foreteeth, pine leaves boiled in vinegar were employed for the relief of toothache. Lung-wort, or the Jerusalem cowslip, was given for lung disease, and water-soldier for gun-shot wounds. The connection between roses and blood is curious. On the continent it is a widespread notion that, if a person is desirous of having ruddy cheeks, he must bury a drop of his blood under a rose bush. As a charm against haemorrhage of every kind, the rose has long been a favourite remedy in Germany. The plants whose leaves bore a fancied resemblance to the moon were regarded with superstitious reverence. Moon-wort was credited by the old alchemists with the power of "curing" quicksilver into pure silver: it could open locks and unshoe such horses as trod upon it. On cutting the roots of the garden flower, Solomon's Seal, some marks are apparent, not unlike the characters of a seal, which induced it to be used for wounds, and receive from the French the name, "l'*herbe de la rupture*" Herbs, either in the dried state or as tinctures and infusions, are not unusual even now in those establishments which display every variety of aromatic and medicinal herb, fossil fruits, fragments of pre-historic root, tertiary blossoms, and dirty receptacles of nondescript scraps and eatables. If these have any virtue what* ever, it undoubtedly must have existed about the Lacustrian period of unwritten human history. They embody, however, much peculiar traditional belief. The herbalist, who sometimes calls himself a "Botanical Practitioner," to his knowledge of plants commonly adds a rough estimate of the credulous part of human nature. He collects "simples," or nature's vegetable remedies, famous from time immemorial. Some, such as camomile and mandrake, have done good service; but usually the influence of Culpepper may be traced in associating with the plants "white magic," such as the phases of the moon and the collocation of the planets. Yet, after all, science does not alter the primeval qualities of plants, and the most skilful men of medical science are the first to recognise the *maxima medicatrix Natura*. The prevalence of poisoning in the Middle Ages caused the concentration of attention upon the deadly drugs and murderous decoctions. There is little doubt but that past ages have discovered secrets in the art that have not been handed down to modern times. Who shall say how many such secrets were known to Friar Laurence, and others such as he, in days when the poison cup was among the recognised forces of diplomacy?

Curing by "sympathy," though its history is very long and very absurd, would seem, by modern investigation, to be capable of beneficial developments. Electro-therapeutics, or the application of static electricity, has become a recognised method. The colour cure in nervous disorders, by which, it is alleged, insane persons are relieved through the influence of red, blue, and violet tints, is agrowing remedial experiment. Psychical methods, without any affectations of mystery or occultism, are of the greatest importance.

The power of music as a medical agency is a typical survival of primitive culture, and a custom which still prevails among uncivilised tribes. The connection of music with the healing art probably originated in the belief that sickness was produced by the influence of evil spirits; one of the ordinary methods of driving these away having been by the effect of music. When pestilences are rife in India "devil- dances" are resorted to, the object being to draw off the bad spirits that cause the plague, and induce them to enter into these wild dancers. Among the Prairie Indians all diseases are treated alike—the expelling of the evil spirit. The medicine-men love to banish the devil of the disease by incantations, gesticulations, and exorcising melody. Apart from this species of superstition, music has held a prominent place in medical treatment both in ancient and modern times. Pythagoras directed certain mental disorders to be cured by its means—a mode of remedy adopted by Xenocrates. Theophrastus argued that the bites of serpents and of other venomous reptiles could be relieved by means of musical sounds. Thallo, when summoned from Crete to Sparta, is said to have checked a disastrous pestilence through the aid of music. Homer represents the Grecian army as employing music to stay the raging of the plague. Aulus Gellius speaks of sciatica being cured by a song; Varso considered singing good for the gout. In later times Descartes alludes to music as a remedy for catalepsy; and Hufeland relates cases of St.Vitus's dance cured by the same means.

Burton, in his "Anatomie of Melancholie," tells us that music is a "sovereign remedy against despair and melancholy—will drive away the Devil himself." Shakespeare mentions music as a remedy for the insanity of Richard II. At the beginning of this century a committee of Continental experts, having made investigation in regard to the relation between music and medicine, reported that music has the power of affecting the whole nervous system so as to give a temporary relief in certain diseases, and even a radical cure. As a striking instance of the peculiar powers of melody, the cure from morbidness effected by Farinelli on Philip of Spain will be remembered. And, indeed, when we reflect how much depends in the case of certain diseases upon the spirits of the patient, it is not surprising that music should oftentimes have been found to exert an exhilarating effect by cheering the mind.

6

FAITH-HEALING AND MEDICINE— (CONTINUED)

"Sympathy"— Whitechapel Atrocities—"Weapon Salve " "Martyrs by Proxy"— The Rosicrucians—Greatrakes and Cagliostro—"Faith Systems"—Medicine Gods— Schools of Doctoring—Micro-organisms—800,000,000- 000,000 Bacilli in Twenty four Hours—Infusoria and Protoplasm—Fission and Spores—Torulae in Wine and Beer—Pasteur and Tyndall—Pyscho-Therapeutics and Electro-Biology—Auto-Suggestion and Mesmerism —Massage and Vaccination —Homeopathy—Nurse- Magnetism—Anti-septic Treatment—Consumption—Is Life a Form of Electricity?

There can be little doubt but that strong "faith" in, or "sympathy" with, a medicine or mode of treatment has often, other circumstances being admitted, produced authenticated cases which puzzle the neurologists. Certainly there must have been something beneficial in the superstition to enable it to maintain its strong hold on the popular, and even the pedant, mind. This mediaeval doctrine of "affinity" is even yet by no means extinct. In some parts of the country the fancy still survives that sickly children can be cured by passing them through split trees, and one of the witnesses in the horrible Whitechapel atrocities expressed her belief in another kind of "sympathy," asserting that, on the day that the crime was committed, she had a presentiment that something had happened to her sister. Reliance in the existence of "sympathies," as I have mentioned, underlaid the medical science, and even the religious instincts of our ancestors, and yet linger among us. Learned men like Lord Bacon and Sir Kenelm Digby wrote on the efficacy of "weapon salve" and the cure of diseases by transferring them into other bodies or substances. It is thought by some that this doctrine of transference may be a reminiscence of the Jewish scapegoat and an explanation of the descent of the "sins of the fathers." There are, at the present day, "martyrs by proxy," who, for a consideration (metallic), profess to be able, by some occult power, to transfer their patients' complaints to themselves. As, in ancient therapeutics, patients were physicked with plants supposed to be in "affinity" with the marks of the diseases, it was by a knowledge of the doctrine that the witch contrived her baneful spells. To destroy a living person it was sufficient to model him or her in wax and expose the effigy to a fire or stick it full of pins. Belief in "sympathy" was an essential of the creed of the Rosicrucians, and modern thought- reading and most of the tales of the apparitions from another world connote it. Some are convinced that there exist people with a peculiar aptitude for receiving supernatural communications. Indeed, Plato's theory of the dual soul has found favour in all generations. Many persons now-a-days would credit the thief-detecting powers of the thought-reader, though they would smile at the ancient test of "the Bible and Key." There are numbers of historical instances of strange presentiments in which some subtle power of sympathy seems to have conveyed the intelligence. Napoleon sent a courier from the battlefield to see whether Josephine was well. Cardan, though at a distance, asserts that he was aware of the execution of his son at Milan. Dr. Johnson relates that a young Irish lord, when a boy at school in France, suddenly stopped his play with the cry, "My father is dead"—the confirming news coming the next day. Probably in all these cases of "sympathetic knowledge" we act, as Lord Bacon says the world does in regard to "prophecies": "Mark when they hit, and never when they miss."

Healing by faith is no novelty. The revival of the idea at the present time is an interesting instance of how certain forms of credulity make periodical struggles for existence, even although the spirit of the age may little favour their pretensions. A noted faith-healer, who professed about two centuries ago to cure diseases by means of stroking, was Valentine Greatrakes. This person was firmly convinced that God had given him the power of healing, and that even the touch of his glove would drive pain and devils away. The Royal Society exposed the quackery. Among many, Joseph Balsamo, popularly known as Cagliostro, was the best known faith-healer of the last century. He professed to heal every disease, to abolish wrinkles, to predict future events, and, in addition, he was a great mesmerist, styling himself "Grand Cophta, Prophet, and Thaumaturge." Carlyle says he had a model face for a quack. Dr. Rock was another panacea professor, no disease baffling him. Dr. Graham, of the Temple of Health, first in the Adelphi, then in Pall Mall, London, also made himself famous. He sold his celebrated "Elixir of Life" for £1,000 a bottle, and was much consulted by all classes. Pfeuffer mentions the faith cures attributed to the prayers of Prince Hohenlohe, who banished maladies by his devoutness. At Knock and other places in Ireland, in Scotland, and many Christian countries abroad, it is believed that the ill and maimed, by witnessing a beatific vision and chewing some of the mortar of the chapel building, can be completely cured. At Eeinsiedeln, in Switzerland, there is a monastery and abbey, the latter of which contains the celebrated "Mother of God," or black image of the virgin, supposed to date from the ninth century. Upon the shrine of the image candles continually burn, and its wonder-working powers are attested by the crutches and other emblems of afflicted humanity heaped together in a corner of the adjacent church. There is a fountain, probably of chemical water, facing the cloister, with twenty-four jets, from each of which the numerous pilgrims are supposed to drink. It is but the other day, one might say, that a faith-healing home known as Bethshan, founded on an interpretation of St. James v. 14, 15, that cures depend on the degree of religious feeling entertained by the sick, was established in London to receive inmates for cure by the exercise of prayer and the anointing with oil.

Thus the point at which we have arrived is, in principle, little beyond the "faith systems" of the savages.

To-day we have our healers, and our believers in disembodied spirits. In pre-historic times it was much the same. Perhaps, in Homer, who represents his heroes as having skill in surgery, we find the earliest mention of the healing art. The worship of the medicine-god, Aesculapius, the physician of the Argonauts, served in its time much the same purpose as the devotional pilgrimages and the health-seeking excursions to "sacred" or chemical springs of a later age. Sick persons slept before the statue of this God, and the remedy was indicated in a dream, the cure of the case being recorded on the walls of the Temple. In the age of Pericles, Hippocrates recognises that disease is a result of violation of natural law, and, the Alexandrian school was successful in anatomy and dissection, assisted in their experiments, no doubt, by the Egyptian practice of disembowelling and embalming the dead. The Romans had a complicated system of superstitious medicine or religion in the treatment of maladies, and the next important advance was the application of physiology to the explanation of disease, by Galen. Byzantine and Arabian medicine was characterised by the intelligent use of metallic compounds and medical plants, the school of Salerno and Paracelsus developing the ideas in mediaeval times. In the seventeenth century the discovery of the circulation of the blood by Harvey, the mechanical philosophy of Descartes, and the introduction of chemical explanations of morbid processes, advanced investigation and accuracy to an immense extent. The iatro-chemical school of Van Helmont, which relied on the use of chemicals; the iatro-physical school of Borelli, which explained the actions and functions of the body chiefly on mechanical principles; and what was afterwards known as the iatro-mathematical school, which reduced the doctors' art to vague theorising, through these causes, were either destroyed or modified. Sydenham, Boerhaave Hoffman, Stahl, Haller, Brown, and others, prepared the way by establishing other theoretical systems, and in this century we find the German savants taking the lead in adapting to medicine the methods of research of physical science.

From the philosophic physicians of centuries ago, who took up and discussed the perplexing problem of the schoolmen as to the time, mode, and place of the introduction of parasites and bacteria into man, modern medicine-men have developed a system which is rapidly revolutionising their whole science. We are just learning the amount of death which humanity takes in with its food and air, and by contact with its species, in the shape of disease germs. Burdon Sanderson has shown "that germs are not so much 'mischief makers' as 'mischief spreaders'" and, considering that bacilli, under favourable conditions, develop to the extent of 800,000,000,000,000 within twenty-four hours, human tissue would be supernaturally pachydermatous to withstand such devastation. Luckily, Pasteur and others, by experimental inoculation, are endeavouring to settle the question of the transmutation of micro-organisms—that is to say, whether, by cultivation or attenuation, they can be checkmated and deprived of their virulent and death- producing qualities.

It used to be thought that decaying matter begot living things. These were known as infusoria, and they were found in water and animal and vegetable substances. There is no doubt now but that these forms of life are not the product of putrid organic matter, but the direct offspring of living things. Thus maggots in rancid meat spring from the living eggs which flies deposit on it. In composition these germs have a curious relation to vitality in the human frame. Protoplasm is a jelly-like substance, which is supposed to be the physical basis of life. It is like egg white, and consists of carbon, hydrogen, oxygen, nitrogen, sulphur, and phosphorus, in proportions which cannot be detected. Generally it is contained in a sort of membrane or cell wall, which can resist acids, alkalies, and moderate heat. But the great characteristic of the stuff is that, though it is without division into organs, it is *formative*, or capable of being transformed into organised material. Of protoplasm all germs are formed. The general name for living cells is microbes, microphytes, or micro-organisms. They are classified by their form—globular, rod-like, thread-like or spiral; and their discovery has given rise to the science of Bacteriology. Some of them, like micrococci, multiply by transverse fission or division— that is, they simply split up, and each half becomes an independent existence, without power of further fission. Bacteria also multiply by division, and, having power of locomotion, they convey diseases and cause most putrefaction and decay. Bacilli grow both by fission and by spore formation. Spores are simply a growth in the protoplasm, which bulges out and bursts into eggs. These organisms are everywhere, and, under favourable conditions of heat, etc., they may multiply by trillions in the course of a few hours, nutriment being obtained from the bodies or things to which they attach themselves.

Haeckel contended that microbes were spontaneously generated; but the experiments of Tyndall and Pasteur have shown that they are invariably the offspring of antecedent life. Fermentation in beer and wine is proved to be accompanied and practically caused by little bodies like bacteria, called torulae, which act by throwing off buds. These organisms, to obtain nourishment, attack the sugar present in the fluid, and, in this way, alcohol and carbonic acid are released. When microbes not natural to the fermentation are introduced, beer and wine become sour or flat. Tyndall applied this theory of fermentation to many diseases. The result has been the discovery of many important bacilli. For instance, there are *anthracis* found in splenetic fever, the *tuberculosis* of consumption, the *rabies* of hydrophobia, the *leprae* of leprosy, the *malariae* of ague, the *comma* of cholera, and those of typhoid fever, erysipelas, haemorrhage, syphilis, scarlatina, and diphtheria, the last being the most recent. A mysterious result of this research is the fact that, if there was no decay and death, no feeding upon chemicals, no poisons, human life and all life would be impossible. It is only when these germs get into their wrong places that they are dangerous. If bacteria find their way into wounds, the result is festering. Surgeons accordingly kill them, and this system is known as the Anti-septic treatment, or Listerism.

Whether diseases are caused by the germs themselves or by their products is a moot point in scientific controversy. Of course, the germ theory is nothing but an advance upon Dr. Jenner's discovery of vaccination. Everyone knows that the antidote to small-pox is the vaccine taken from cattle suffering from cow-pox. This is inoculated usually by means of a lancet, that it may circulate in the blood, and produce a mild condition of small-pox. In this case the poison is introduced in anticipation of and as protective against the disease. Pasteur has introduced the system of attenuation of the virus, and others that of the cultivation, in order to check a disease in progress. The virus is passed through the systems of many animals until it is sufficiently robbed of its virulence. It is then inserted with a syringe. Science is not prepared to say why inoculation is successful; but the explanation is hazarded that certain bacilli are produced, which are capable of resisting or neutralising the germs causing the malady. Homeopathy—the theory that disease is cured by remedies which produce on a healthy person effects similar to the symptoms of complaint under which the patient suffers—is the basis of the new departure. Epidemic diseases are the effect of organisms which have sprung and spread from parasitic life in the dust, water, and air that surround us. Although these fungoid decayers are necessary to healthy life, cure can only result by their destruction when they are "out of place." It is possible that an age of purity could be attained, were some means discovered to isolate ourselves and our belongings from the ravages of these microscopic highwaymen.

The connection of medical discovery with legislation and politics is of sufficient importance to be treated at length in the article which I entitle "Sin and Crime." How far is a criminal responsible for a deed which, owing to a diseased nervous system, he has committed without moral guilt? How much of the so-called premeditated law-breaking is a result of insanity—of mania undefined, and not understood? But this is only a type of the mysterious difficulties with which medical science has to contend. As civilisation advances new diseases arise, notwithstanding improvement in the environment of existence. Many forms of disease, such as kleptomania and consumption, are to be found only in cultured communities. In regard to the latter, there are over 200,000 sufferers in this country, and each year about 70,000 die from it. And it is found that lung maladies are on the increase. In Germany the whole subject of phthisis has received great attention since Koch and Klein suggested the use of the surgeon's knife. It seems that incisions can be made actually into the lungs as a means of cure. Doctors differ widely in their theories as to consumption. Koch, who by inoculating animals with germs gave them the disease, originated the bacillian theory. Hambledon, a specialist, at a British Association meeting denied that bacilli were the cause, and the controversy inspired Dr. Evans to write the following impromptu:—

> "To cure all diseases the Health-god of old
> Used a serpent-twined staff, or *bacillum*, to hold;
> But the modern physician regards us as silly
> If we doubt that diseases all spring from bacilli.
> Thus, that which of old used to heal and to save,
> Now by phthisis and fever conducts to the grave."

The opponents of the bacteriologists argue that more regard should be taken of broad nostrils than broad chests. Among savages, with their free, open-air life, consumption is practically unknown. Disuse of the lungs or breathing organs under the modern conditions of life, which arc artificial and restricted, produce phthisical patients. For years the insurance companies decided to take narrow chests as the test of consumption. That is now abandoned, for the army medical statistics have shown that the tallest and strongest men are generally liable to the malady. Testimony given by adepts at Lord Dunraven's excellent Committee on the "Sweating System" tends to confirm the fact that the source of the insidious disease is rather to be sought in the improper conditions of life than in any hereditary predisposition. It is true that congenital influence is a prevailing cause. But we have it on authority that improved sanitation might reduce mortality from phthisis by one-half. Dr. Squire states that tailors arc specially liable to consumption, their mortality being one-fourth compared with one- tenth for the whole population of London. The obvious inferences arc, of course, that excessive indoor employment, insufficiency of food and fresh air, and the injury resulting from the mechanical conduct of labour are the main aggravating agencies, more especially in persons with unhealthy predispositions.

No less striking, and little less new, are the innovations of recent years in the art of treatment and applying remedies. Medicine is passing from its Preventive to its Reformative stage. The influence of the mind upon the bodily health is the most accepted postulate. The idea of "sympathetic" curing is undergoing an avatar. Writers of such responsibility as Liebault, Bernheim, Braid, Haek Tuke, and Richet are not averse to treatment by psycho-therapeutics, which is simply a scientific form of a very old superstition. It is well known that a dreaming person will dream, and even act in the state of sleep, that which is whispered into the ear. Dreaming is merely the mimicry by the *automatic* portion of the brain —the central ganglia—of that which the *intellectual* portion, when awake, has thought, imagined, or done. Somnambulism is but putting the dream in action by the concentrated power of the automatic ganglia. Mesmerism or hypnotism, again, is merely induced sleepwalking, a result of subduing the intellectual portion of the brain, in order that the mechanical—the ganglia— uncontrolled by the intellect, may be subject to the influence of suggestion from another mind after the manner of the dreaming person.

The Nancy school of medicine believe in the power of suggestion *(i.e.,* suggesting to the patient that he should get well, etc.) when the patient is in the somnolent or hypnotic state. And faith-healing in this sense has become popular as a therapeutic agent, not only for the relief of so- called nervous and fanciful complaints, but for the cure of disease, though many practitioners agree that, in most cases and diseases, the ordinary anaesthetics will never be supplanted. The use of Franklinism, or medical galvanism, has prompted the establishment of special hospitals where nerve excitation and muscular manipulation, otherwise known as massage, in the hands of nurse- electricians, claim to do the work of drugs. Mr. Weir Mitchell, of America, whose book, "Fat and Blood," revives this very ancient system, repudiates all idea of moral or mental massage; yet, when he suggests that the vital principle may be a condition of animal electricity, generated by the friction of the stream of blood against the coats of the arteries, we are inclined to dispute his medical psychology.

There is nothing new in the idea of electro-biology. It was an old magical belief that a loadstone, because it attracts steel, will draw away pain, "the iron of the soul," from the body; and, now-a-days, many a peasant carries a magnet in his pocket as a preservative against rheumatism and the like, as others will wear galvanic bandages. In the future life may outrun its Scriptural span; but the evolution of such a result will be the seed-bed of many an unheard-of superstition. Perhaps, on the whole, Dryden was not far wrong when he wrote:—

> "The first physicians by debauch were made;
> Excess began and sloth sustains the trade.
> The wise for cure on exercise depend;
> God never made his work for man to mend."

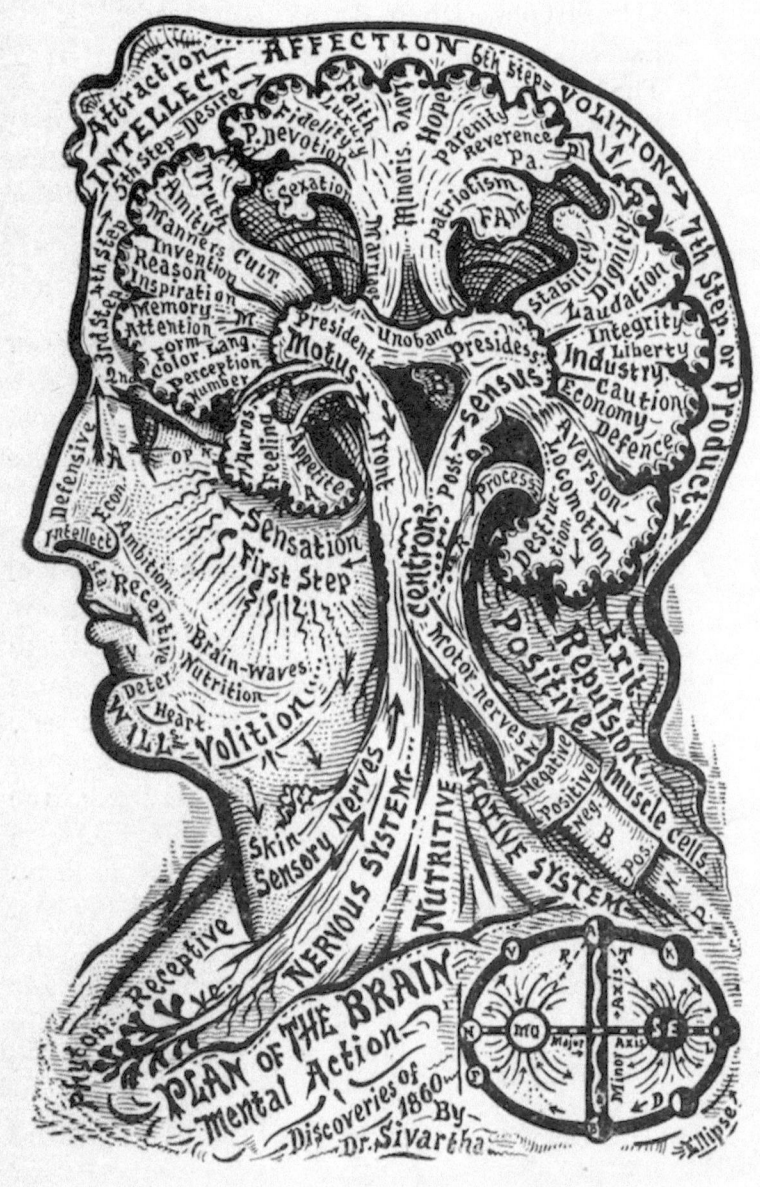

7

THEOSOPHY: ANCIENT AND MODERN

The Cabala—Prehistoric People—"Revealer of Sacred Things"—Temple Secrets—Ancestor and Animal Wor- ship—Divine Essence—Mystical Swooning—Fakirs and Dervishes—Supersensuousness—"Buddha's Night"— The Nous—Hebraic Sephiroth—Heavenly Men—Is God Nothing?—The Victorines and "Gottesfreunde"— Is God a Female?—Hegel and Spinoza—Philosophic Quackeries — "Inner light"—Spirit-Doctrines—The Abecedarians — Unio Mystica—Madame Blavatsky and Mahatmaism—Neo-Theosophy.

From the earliest times to the latest, religious creeds and cults have always claimed a *Cabala,* or Kabbalah—that is to say, a secret body of traditional knowledge handed down from age to age only to the initiated. This wisdom was usually conveyed orally. Creuzer and others, owing to the prevalence of this esoteric element, have been led to conclude that all faiths and sects are but the echoes conveyed in an allegorical and symbolical form of some original race of the highest culture, concerning whom we have lost all traces. And M. Bailly, arguing upon the same lines, contends that the origin of all our sciences is lost with the memory of this prehistoric people. It is pointed out how the pagan Greeks were of opinion that all the truths and moralities contained in the Christian writers were embodied in the Eleusinian mysteries. The meaning of these was explained to the qualified initiates by the *Revealer of Sacred Things.* Christian writers have done their best to misrepresent these rites. They have charged them with the immoralities which were the features of the Orphic and Phrygian mysteries. But research has shown that the ritual was based upon religious myths, and that no secret was kept from the initiated. The early races also always possessed temple secrets, which only the faithful could grasp. Every letter, word, number of the Mosaic law is significant in a mysterious manner to the Jewish Rabbins. The essence of Christianity is "belief," the necessary passport to illumination. There is not a new idealism nor spiritual nor psychical clique without "faith" as the memorandum of association and essential postulate. Whatever this secret thing—this exclusive wisdom—only imparted to the elect can be, its manifestations have been of the most versatile and varied character. Theosophy, magic, religions, astrology, alchemy and philosophy, with their minor and major offshoots, have all been attempts to apply a Cabala— attempts which rather multiply than decrease as the world gets older. In the myths and legends which, in one form or another, have reached us from ante-history times, our savants for years have sought for the source- Wisdom, from which everything of intellectual interest has eddied and ebbed. Voss, in his "Anti-Symbolik," and Lobeck in his "Aglaophamus," have destroyed and exploded all the *a priori* theories that the mysteries and folk-lore enshrined a primitive revelation of Divine truth, or that ever a superiorly-cultured race with a monopoly of wisdom existed at all within immemorial time. It would seem that the germ of truth in all speculations concerning the original Cabala was correctly stated by Plutarch, who lays it down that it requires a philosophic and religious training with balance and without bias to understand truth in its highest forms.

Theosophy in its vaguest sense means the greatest wisdom. Among the barbarians it left the forms of ancestor and animal worship, and developed into one or other phase of Pantheism. As applied to advanced systems of religious thought, there are many connotations. It may mean insight into the Divine nature and processes, either as a result of some higher faculty, or of some supernatural revelation to the individual. It may propose a theory which is not based upon any special illumination, but is simply put forward as the deepest speculative wisdom of the author. Or it may be a miserable mysticism—a sort of aesthetic heathenism with mazes of misty words of thoughts, compounded of plagiarisms from Oriental systems with dashes of supernatural science, and mixed, parenthesized, and annotated into unintelligibility. Theosophic theories usually start with the assumption of a Divine essence, of which an explanation is offered. An attempt is then made to deduce the phenomenal universe from the play of forces within the Divine nature itself. Or the contrary plan may be adopted. From analysis of phenomena the knowledge of the existence and nature of God is arrived at, this of course being a distinctly philosophic method.

The object aimed at is to prove that the human mind, though finite, is capable of grasping the Divine essence; though infinite, of understanding the ultimate reality of things, and enjoying actual communication with God. In some of the forms this mysticism maintains direct intercourse with the Great Supreme Indwelling Power of the Universe, without such media as spirits, revelations, oracles, answers to prayers; but by a species of ecstatic transformation making the believer a "partaker of Divine Nature," and God not an object, but an experience. A faculty above reason, by which man can be placed in complete union with God—a union in which the consciousness of self has disappeared—is assumed. This faculty is variously known as ecstasy, intuition, mystical swooning, inspiration, and appears alike among the Hindoos, the Neo-Platonists, the mediaeval Christian saints, and some modern coteries, such as Spiritualists and fanatic pietists. The Indian Fakirs and Mohammedan Dervishes by long practice have obtained a marvellous power of concentration, the physiological reasons of which will be found in the article on "Occult Forces." They can at will produce a state of hypnotism shown by mental exaltation and complete unconsciousness of their surroundings. While so absorbed, they will endure pains which, in their normal state, would cause fearful agony. Buddhist devotees, and indeed many fanatics of all fancies, can attain by a sort of auto-suggestion a foretaste of Nirvana, or a condition of trance, ecstasy, or beatific vision. It may be noted that, if such a faculty existed, God is degraded to a mere object of sense, and knowledge of him is a state of brutish torpor and unnatural excitation. Yet this metaphysical theory of the *supersensuous*, in which all self-consciousness is lost—a mere morbid development of sense or nerve-melancholy, resulting from an overdriven brain—is received with assent by some of the unlettered philosophies of the day which profess to be Christian.

Such speculation is commonly the out-growth of many different thoughts and feelings. It is a natural re-action against meaningless ceremony in an attempt to develop the human heart. Brahminism and Buddhism both teach this mystical absorption by the One Power, and the consequent lack of value of the human personality. Buddha showed how man, from his inner mental make and desires, and from his external troubles and fatalities, must suffer till he ceases to live or succeeds in uniting himself with the Immanent. Only by a supreme effort of concentrated meditation, asceticism and virtue, and the destruction of all desire for material or immaterial existence here or hereafter, can the sage ever attain peace. This is the earthly Nirvana, the blissful foretaste of the grander Nirvana enjoyed by the perfect in the next world. The bad, the self-sufficient, must plunge again into the storms and vortices of existence till they purify and escape into the silent shore of "Buddha's night." In the third century we find Neo-Platonism attempting to steal from the ideal, supernatural, and mystical elements of Plato's thoughts, from heathenism, from Oriental superstition, and from Christianity, the constituents which would frame a new, true, and universal religion. It was a philosophic theology and Pantheistic eclecticism, which sought to reconcile Polytheism with Monotheism, superstition with culture, and the old faith with refined and idealised theosophy. The mediaeval Church borrowed many of the ideas of this speculation, elaborated by Plotinus, from the suggestiveness of the "Attic Moses"—Plato. It is declared that the One Power transcends existence and emanates from itself *vous*, which constitutes our ideas, the mind, or the intelligible world. The soul is the emanation or offshoot of this *vous*, or mind derived from God, and, by its motion, begets matter. Man accordingly, to reach the state of identification with God, must leave all his thought behind, for re-union with the Deity is not so much knowledge as ecstasy or inspired enthusiasm. The elaborate esoteric system of theosophy the Jews propounded in the tenth century, under the name of "Kabbalah," is also found permeating the mediaeval Church.

First of all, the idea of the reception of their doctrines in an unbroken chain by tradition through the prophets and patriarchs is dwelt upon. Of this the apostolic succession of the Catholic Church is an imitation. God, in Hebraic theogony, is above everything, and made manifest by Sephira or Emanations or Intelligences, or spiritual substances. There were ten of these Sephiroth— wisdom, beauty, foundation, and the like. The Archetypal or primordial and heavenly man, who is double- natured, being finite and infinite, is composed of them. From these Sephiroth also proceeds the universe, which is not created from nothing, but is the expansion or evolution of the Sephiroth. Hence everything—spirit and body—must return to the source from which it emanated, and nothing can be annihilated. This doctrine or this secret wisdom is contained in the Hebrew Scriptures, in the "Book of Creation," and in the "Zokar." But the uninitiated cannot perceive it, because they have not "faith," and because they are not spiritually-minded!

The Christian Church about this time also preached that the return to God is the consummation of all things. For God, being above all comment or category, is not improperly called Nothing—a nothing or an incomprehensible essence, out of which all things are created. We find Bernard of Clairvaux advocating, as a sort of protest against the neglect of the spirit of religion, asceticism, on the ground that St. Paul saw his ecstatic vision because he became dead to the body of the world. The Victorines, following the lead of Hugo of St. Victor, contended, in opposition to dialectical theology, that the objects of religious contemplation are partly above and partly contrary (as the Trinity) to the reason. Later the worldliness of the Church and the scandalous lives of the clergy prompt a theology of the heart, and the German mystics rally round monkism and the esoteric, supported in their rebellion by such prophetic visions as that of Hildegard of Bingen. The sceptical spirit, thus introduced by those who did not feel the need of philosophising their beliefs, has never left the Church. Eckhart, about 1270, stamped the note of mediaeval mysticism. He asserted the transcendentalism which ever since has clung to German metaphysic. The Godhead, he insisted, is a dark and formless essence, and, to know God, it is needful by self-abnegation to become ignorant of ourselves and everybody else. This self-annihilation is the only means of attaining re-union with or "burial in" God. The *Gottesfreunde* or Society of the Friends of God strove to establish this *unio mystica*—this loving intercourse with Deity. Boehme carried the theosophy to such a length that he hastened the advent of the Reformation. He mixed his theology with magical science, and diluted it with heathen scholasticism. Madame Blavatsky owes almost all her mock science to his writings. His object was to reconcile the existence and the might of evil with the goodness of God. The *mysterium magnum* or "eternal nature" lies in God, which is as the negative to the positive. That is to say, God is the father of things and the eternal nature of God, the *matrix*, the mother of things—an idea of which Mr. Laurence Oliphant has made considerable use in the theogonising of his Divine Feminine.[1] The cosmogony is a strained Paracelsian symbolism, which has been adopted by Schelling, Boeder, Swedenborg, and such dreamers.

It is usually accepted that Theosophy differs from Pantheism in that its object is religious, while the latter is a mere system of resolving all things into one metaphysical power or substance. But it may be well to mention in this review that the "speculative" or "absolute" philosophies, such as those of Hegel and Spinoza, proceed deductively from the idea of God. From this aspect the universe is regarded as the evolution of the Divine nature—God being no more than the principle of Unity immanent in the whole. There is certainly a Pantheistic suggestion about such systems, and it may be taken that Theosophy, as a rule, is distinguished by regarding God as the transcendent source of being and purity, from which man, whose aim is to unite himself with his source, in his natural state is alienated.

It is notable that in the intervals between each scientific advance there spring up numberless religions or philosophic quackeries, which profess to clear up all phenomena inexplicable at the time by the laws of nature. This is doubtless due to the tendency of human thought to re-act against the positiveness of reason. We have been in such a period of rebellion since German transcendentalism made its influence wide-felt. There is a renascence of the spirit of wonder—a mood of expectant attention, nurtured by doubt and uncertainty, and distinguished by moral weakness and indulgent egoism. In religious communities a feeling prevails on the one hand that the spirit is lost in the predominance of form, and, upon the other, that what we require is more symbolism and superstition than ever in order to check an unprofitable and a dangerous socialism of the soul. Consequently, we find ecclesiasticism or dogmatic religion gaining ground among some classes of the orthodox, and Salvationism and the Evangelical absorbing most of those who do not compromise with their surroundings, and become indifferent. Among the first order the influence of the Kabbalah may be detected—an influence which seems to be establishing a species of Christianised Neo-Platonism. In the camp of the latter, under the guise of spiritualising theology— an object claimed by both—a revival of the chemico-·astrological speculation of Paracelsus is apparent. The dignified ritual of the High Church, with its superstitious ceremonies, scripture-worship, and esoteric indefiniteness, is as distinctive of the times as the religiosity of the Quakers, with their doctrines of the "inner light" and the mystical influence of the spirit. Naturally the minnows and mimics of learning are active in turn. The vulgarities of Atheism, the plagiarists of classic philosophy or pagan fancy, the revivers of spirit-doctrines and meteorological psychology, and the "inspirationalism" of Oriental wonder-wisdom wage, in their own way, distressful war in the lesser sphere, which revolves round the "light and leading" of the age. To such a baneful extent does this prostituted dialectic proceed that one is inclined to wish with Bakunin, the Russian Nihilist, that all science and art were abolished, that men might live like brothers, in a state of "holy and wholesome ignorance. " It was such a state of things, no doubt, which led the Anabaptist Abecedarians to deny the value of all human learning, even the ABC. lest it should clog the track leading towards Divine truth.

Each and all of the "new" theories and nonsenses which profess to be advances on the theosophies of thousands of years ago are distinguished by that ostentatious omniscience which is almost invariably the accompaniment of ignorance. Muddle up a mass of modern popularised science with some late symbolical guesses at crude old myths; dabble in sententious quotations; rarely encounter a problem without digging for antiquated analogies to meet it, and mix the whole with philosophic taplash and mock sociology, and you may safely begin business as a "Prophet, " or "Mahatma, " or "Diviner, " or what you please. It is woful that our incomplete knowledge of ether and electricity and anthropology prevent the application of the same searching analysis to which other prehistoric myths have been subjected, to the so-called occult or perhaps occidental sciences.

As a typical instance of these mushroom supernaturalisms which come into prominence amid the present-day antagonism between fact and faith—the perplexity resulting from irreconcilable aspects of truth and the scientific tendency of spiritualising life—I could not select anything better than the Pseudo-Theosophy made familiar, theatrically, by Madame Bla\atsky. Here is a doctrine borrowed from Buddhism and Zoroastrianism. It appropriates the central idea of Paganism and Christianity alike—that of the *unio mystica*, the attainment in contemplation of the union of the soul with God—mixes this up with calm contradiction of scientific certitude, and substitutes a delirious transcendental clap-trap. From an old monk or Lama, residing in a monastery in the mountain range of Altyn-Toga, in Thibet, who possesses the "Book of Dzyan," and the secret literature of all wisdom, Madame gets a glimpse of an archaic manu script, a collection of palm-leaves made impermeable to water, fire, and air by some specific unknown process. And, on the strength of this, she bases a philosophy of phrases founded upon often less than half-knowledge of facts, propounds a mythical cosmic origin, traverses the chief positions of modern science and metaphysic, and asks us to believe in the resultant of a number of guesses and proposals drawn from all quarters, and strung together into an esoteric system. She writes a book called "The Secret Doctrine," which is an expository compilation of Eastern occultism—a work which undoubtedly stamps her as a scholar of great ability. In this we find the old fruitless methods adopted—pseudo- logical deduction from abstract conceptions, from *a priori* assumptions and self-evident axioms. This plausible reasoning is made imposing by throwing it into a sort of syllogistic symposium or mathematical shapes, after the manner of the Wolfians, who presented theology in the semblance of geometry. Our "faith" is called into exercise at the outstart. Thus, at once, we are precipitated amid notions that have the advantages of the sandals of Theramenes, which fit any feet. We must believe in the "Cabala" of the phantasy, and our scepticism estops our attainment of wisdom. There is a *Higher*

Science (these facts I learn from some excellent Theosophical pamphlets written by Mr. William Kingsland) than that of matter. "It is religion in its true sense, and deals with the hidden forces in nature, at which physical science stops short." This superlative science knows everything, and is to be appreciated only by the exercise of the *supersensuous* faculties. I have already shown how this old-world assumption offensively degrades God. The way to discover these powers is to become a Mahatma or Initiate or Adept in the wonder-wisdom buried in the Thibetan oasis. This is done by exhausting one's own Karma or Fate, and by becoming master of oneself. Equal and adequate training of the physical, mental, and spiritual natures together, be it known, with the credulous or "faith" side of man, is sure to attain this result. Occult science tells you in advance, as the savage could have done in regard to the ghost-souls, that you can separate the whole consciousness from the physical body, alienate sense from spirit—the only real thing. When a man is able to do this *voluntarily* he is able to transcend matter, or live seemingly in a state of prolonged dreamland. A physiologist would say that the brain of the Theosophist is playing him tricks, because, as in dreams, the automatic ganglia are only mimicing the intellectual or psychomotor centres when they are inactive in sleep. When you have transferred your personality to this loftier plane, where you are lost in the vortices of cuckoo- cloudland, far from fogs, tax-gatherers, piano-organs, and cats'-meat-men, the physical state is no longer necessary. In life we have arrived at the state in which the soul is after death, and this we are to call "Devachan." When we are acclimatised within the sphere of the spirit "the earthly paradise" for a termless period of probation, we are entitled to become Initiates or Mahatmas, and to possess wieldless power, see like a clairvoyant through "astral light," and defy time, distance, and space.

While these higher principles, which we are told *do* exist, and apart from matter, are developing to maturity we shall have arrived at a state of enthusiastic fanaticism, where Madame becomes our prophet. You must not notice that Madame has fallen into the common trap of working upon spiritual facts with physical categories. You must listen to the commonplace of all speculations, that Theosophy has had a lengthy past, its ages being seven. In these ether, dynamics, and

Keely's motor have played great parts. There are also seven cosmical elements, either because, I suppose, there are seven planets, or because the root-word, "seva," both in Arabic and Hebrew, denotes completion or complement. Of these, four are material, the fifth, ether, is "semi-material," and the seventh "as yet absolutely beyond the range of human perception," and, may I add, the All-Wisdom. The Absolute is the One-All, and cannot be described —it can only be symbolised. Possibly, when the nature and constitution of the seventh element is discovered, we shall learn. This is practically the whole creed, which is but a borrowed obscurantism, a designed darkening of what every one wants to understand. As Byron said of Coleridge's metaphysics, it is the fault of Blavatskyism that the seer neglects to explain her explanations.

Votaries are secured just according to the success in inducing metaphysical disease. The method is an abnormal development of emotional and superstitious natures in an overpressed pursuit of nebulous ideals. Like Montanism, the practical morality is absurdly and morbidly overstrained, and its only praiseworthy element is the enforcing of self-abnegation, in which it is at one with the *Yog-vidya* in India and every other sect. For the rest, Neo-theosophy may be left to the Philistines and the poets.

> "Then in sweet Theosophic employment
> Shall Labour find food and content,
> While plutocrats scorn self-enjoyment,
> And landlords refrain from their rent;
> All laws shall be laid in abeyance,
> For the world shall roll free on its course
> In a blissful Anarchical *séance*,
> A rapture of Psychical Force!"

---

1. See chapter on "Religion and Religions."

8

DEATH

Skeletons and Funereal Insignia—The "Dance of Death"—Eccentricities of Dying Celebrities—Domine, Domine Fac Finem—Churchyards—Death by Hanging and "Adam's Apple"—The Last Living Thing—Ceremony of Conclamation—Facies Hippocratica—Theological Theory of Disease—Predictions by the Dying—Is Death a Pain?—Burial Alive—Decisive Tests of Death?—Corpse- Physiology— Whence?

Is death a state midway between the consciousness of life and utter annihilation, or is it nothing but annihilation—complete destruction of body and soul? Whether, as matter is indestructible, mind, dependent on matter is indestructible also or the reverse? Whether soul has an existence altogether impossible in that which is material? This is the great mystery which each can only penetrate by individual experience. "There is nothing," says Montaigne, "of which I am so inquisitive as the manner of men's deaths, their dying words, their dying looks, their deportment. A register of the deaths of various people, with notes, would be of use in instructing men both to live and to die."

It was the custom of the ancient Egyptians to hang up, even at their feasts, a skeleton to remind them of the uncertainty of life. Ignorance in regard to the conditions upon which the spirit of vitality leaves its mortal tabernacle has produced fictitious terrors among most peoples. Death depicted as the universal destroyer and the gloomy symbolism of hearses, cross-bones, skulls, mattocks, and other funereal *insignia*, are the calm- inspiring hideosities inculcated unluckily by Christian conceptions of a climax which is simply the unconscious extinction of the vital principle. Visual representations of the Destroyer became common after the spread of Christianity, and monkism favoured the awful symbol of the skeleton as a popular effigy. This religious terrorism was followed by *grotesquerie*, which made the skeleton the subject of burlesque and mockery, like the mediaeval allegories in picture and drama known by the description, the "Dance of Death." Of a less dreadful character, indeed, were the superstitions of heathens, for for them death was at least a Nirvana, which, if not desirable, was environed with poetic aspirations. The expiring Manfred, in Byron's gloomy dramatic poem, bids the old man mark that "it is not so difficult to die." And, indeed, the inordinate fear of death which prevails so largely is in much degree due to the failure to distinguish between the phenomena of disease and the phenomena which indicate the approach of death. Meditation on an event which is deemed an evil engenders the sickening forebodings which needlessly disrupt the serenity of the human mind. Even Dr. Johnson, strongly intellectual as he was, wrote to Dr. Taylor: "Oh, my friend, the approach of death is very dreadful;" and, in a conversation with Dr. Hawkins, he confessed "he never had a moment in which death was not terrible to him." But a crowning proof of the constitutional superstition which would delay death may be seen in the story which describes the Doctor having once been much relieved from his dropsical pains by incisions made into his leg, as seizing a pair of scissors and plunging them into the calf of each leg. How often has an indulgence in a morbid apprehension hastened the end of life? Marshal Biron, the intrepid, on his death-bed gave way to "womanish tears and raging imbecility;" and Erasmus, the virtuous, miserably groaned out, "*Do mi tie, Domine fac finem*" It is not our hopes beyond the grave which cause this awe; they are of a higher character. It is the fear, which physiological principles have proved to be, in general, fallacious, of enduring physical pangs in the act of dying.

Churchyards were originally made, by the decree of Lycurgus, near the temples of religious worship, that the multitudes which proceed thither to devotion by the sight of tombstones and graves should lessen the sting of the knowledge of death. Yet the end has been met with reckless temerity on not a few occasions, especially where the scaffold has exacted its due. Sir Thomas More, on ascending the scaffold, which was of a feeble structure, remarked jocularly to Kingston: "I pray you, Master Lieutenant, see me safe up, and for my coming down let me shift for myself;" and to the executioner: "My neck is so short, strike not awry for the saving of thy honesty." Of course, an affectation of dying with *eclat* is not unusual with criminals; but many of the brave and unfortunate have encountered death without fear. The Duke D'Enghien, condemned by Bonaparte to be shot, advised the grenadiers to lower their arms, "otherwise you will miss or only wound me;" and Marshal Ney, who was shot in the gardens of the Tuilleries, desired the soldiers to take a sure aim at his heart. King Charles II., in his last moments, felt bound to apologise to his courtiers for having been such an unconscionable time in dying. Religious resignation has undoubtedly frequently produced a calm contemplation of approaching death. But equal intrepidity has been displayed where sacred sentiment was entirely lacking. Cloots, the Atheistical French revolutionist, who called himself the "orator of the human race," becoming a "suspect" to Robespierre, was condemned, and on his way to the guillotine discoursed on Materialism and the contempt of death. On the scaffold he begged the executioner to behead him last, that he might make some observations essential to the establishment of certain scientific principles while the heads of the others were falling!

It has become pretty well known that life never departs without some material change having taken place in the body. When the laws which maintain the relation between the bodily organs are suspended, disease ensues, and the brain and nerves cease to command the motion of the limbs; the heart cannot propel the blood, the lungs cease to perform their functions, and death occurs. Neither brain, heart, nor lungs is the seat of vitality; their combined action constitutes life. Marie Antoinette, during the Reign of Terror, was dead from a blow by a mulatto before her head was cut off: concussion of the brain stopped the action of the heart. In severer shocks of the nervous system the action of all the vital organs is simultaneously suspended, and death is instantaneous. Livy says that, when Hannibal had conquered the Romans at Cannae, two women, seeing their sons whom they had thought dead return in health, died immediately from excessive joy. The heiress of Leibnitz dropped down dead on finding herself in the possession of a large fortune. Ludovicus Vives relates that a French Jew came safely in the dark over a dangerous passage; the next day, on viewing where he had crossed, he fell dead. Montaigne relates the case of a German nobleman who died suddenly on hearing that his son had fallen in battle. Besides shocks to the nervous system, violent mental emotions sometimes give rise to insanity or idiocy; and, when death is induced by any disease primarily commencing in the brain, heart, and lungs, the other organs will perform their functions, even though the patient be in a state of profound insensibility. The brain, in its superior region, indeed, is thought to be endowed with less sensibility than any of the other vital organs, and it may be sliced away to a considerable extent without producing pain, and seemingly without any injury to animal life. Cases are on record in which cavities were found on dissection in the brains of individuals who had lived in the enjoyment of good health and intellect. It may be interesting here to correct the erroneous popular belief that criminals who are hanged die from the spinal marrow being injured by dislocation of the neck. Death by hanging, however, is physiologically produced by the compression of the thyroid cartilage in front of the neck, vulgarly called "Adam's apple." A tube introduced into the wind-pipe below the rope may preserve life. Strange to say, sudden death is much more frequently caused by affections of the heart than by diseases of the brain; but the essentials of death are that each of the vital organs should cease to perforin their functions.

The phenomena presented in death depend very much on the order in which brain, heart, and lungs—the "tripod of life"—relinquish their functions. All deaths may be thus divided: —First, those which result from sudden shocks and poisons, occasioning the immediate suspension of the action of brain, heart, and lungs, the body dying from the centre to the extremities. Secondly, those which result from diseases, which by degrees exhaust the vital powers, the body dying from the extremities to the centre. The last living thing that dies within us is the *ultmium moriens,* or right auricle of the heart, which receives the tainted blood after its circulation through the body. The sense of sight usually fails before that of speech; and the power of hearing often remains after all the other functions appear to be entirely suspended. On account of this latter fact the Romans and other nations established the ceremony of *conclamation* in calling by name three times the person supposed to be dead. Cesalpinas states that this was done to prevent the burial of persons only apparently dead. Hence, when all is over, the Romans cried, *Conclamatum est*— The deceased has been called. The "wake" in Ireland is a similar custom—one which, according to Bruhier, is not unknown in France. It would seem, then, that the dying may hear, long after the power of acknowledging the fact has gone, the unavailing expressions of grief uttered by those around the death-bed.

Hippocrates, in determining the signs of coming death after acute diseases, dwells on the character of the physiognomy. The nose becomes sharp, the eyes hollow, the temples collapsed, the cars cold and contracted, the lobes inverted, the skin on the forehead hard and dry, and the whole face assumes a palish green, a black, livid, or leaden hue. In the schools of medicine at the present day this, which is referred to as the *Fades Hippocratica* (and correctly described by Shakespeare at the decease of Falstaff), is held to be sufficient proof of the approach of death. The nose becomes sharp, because the muscles of the face have lost their power and the nostrils fall in; the eye becomes hollow, because the fat in its orbit upon which it rested has shrunk; the face, lips, tips of the fingers, and toes assume a pallor, because the blood is no longer stimulated by the lungs.

The influence of the mind in quickening or retarding the coming of death, in many cases accounts for the presentiments of a fatal termination which some patients prophetically entertain. The modern medical treatments known as Electro-Massage and Psycho-Therapeutics or Faith-Healing, depend largely on this fact of the influence of the mind on the heart's action. The theological theory of disease, that maladies were punishments or judgments of God, and that they were to be cured by miracles, by devotion to relics, and by simple prayer to the Almighty—though opposed to sanitary science—has assisted in saving many lives. At this day, within the Continental churches, a common feature is the number of votive offerings that cluster round the image of a favourite saint by those who believe they have successfully supplicated their intervention. A case is recorded of a person in Paris who had been sentenced to be bled to death; but, instead of the punishment being actually inflicted, he was merely induced to believe it was so, by water, while his eyes were blinded, being trickled down his arm. This mimicry so completely depressed the action of the heart that the man lost his life. Another unfortunate person had been condemned to be beheaded, and the moment his neck was adjusted on the block a reprieve arrived; but the victim was already sacrificed— the fear of the axe having done what its fall would have done. Drs. Cheyne and Baynard mention the case of Colonel Townsend, "who could die, and yet by an effort, or somehow, could come to life again." The Colonel ultimately never revived on an occasion of showing this peculiar power. Celsus knew a priest who could separate himself from his senses when he liked and die like a dead man.

One of the most curious problems is the clearing up of the mind previous to death and the predictions often made by dying persons. Arotoeus noted this especially in persons who had died of brain-fever. There is no occasion, according to Sir Henry Halford and others, to attribute the circumstance to any preternatural cause. Immediately before death the heart beats strongly and the respiration is hurried. The blood, in consequence, in passing through the lungs, becomes more perfectly oxygenised than ordinarily, and is in that state transmitted with accelerated force through the brain, which, being subjected to a high stimulus, renews its functions with great vigour. Thus the vivid recollection, the clear reasoning, and shrewd sensibility manifested by many on the death-bed is explained. In respect, however, to the predictions of death, it is feared that we know too little of the conditions and relations of the human mind to be able to state more than that the concentrated energies of the patient may take cognisance of events and objects to others imperceptible. Powerful mental emotions, indeed, induce such states. Under the influence of fear the distressed often became immovable, deaf, and blind to all appeals.

A great question is whether, at the moment of death, the dying suffer pain? That persons suffering from sickness suffer pain, there is no doubt; but such pain is a result of disease. Yet it seems that we must distinguish between the pain of disease and the act of dying. It is popularly imagined that there is a strange reluctance of the spirit to leave the body. The fact is, nevertheless, that the powers of suffering are enfeebled and the capacities of pain almost exhausted. The groans and convulsions of the sufferer are not necessarily indicative of pain, since they occur in epilepsy, apoplexy, hysteria, and other convulsive fits, from which the person recovers without recollection of having endured them.

The ordinary signs of death—prostration, lividity, coldness, and the commencement of putrefaction—often occur when the person is still capable of being revived. The body of a drowned person, notwithstanding the failure of a mirror applied to the mouth to catch the breath, or a feather on the lips to indicate expiration— both of which are erring as decisive tests—is frequently resuscitated. Respiration, depending on the action of the heart, may, as in syncope, be for a time suspended. Persons in a trance, owing to the contracted heart depriving the brain of blood, present the appearance of death, and unluckily from this cause such have been frequently buried alive. Lancisi, the physician of Pope Clement XI., reported that during the plague many persons were thus interred. Everyone knows the story of Vesalius, the father of anatomy, who, on dissecting a woman supposed to have died in a hysterical fit, found, on making the first incision, by her motions and cries that she was still alive. Forced by the indignation of his countrymen to fly, Vesalius died of hunger in Spain. Howard, in his book on Prisons, quotes cases of criminals supposed to be dead from gaol-fever who recovered; and Dr. Gordon has observed that in times of public sickness, especially in warm climates where speedy interment is necessary, many persons have been entombed alive.

There are but three conclusive signs of the arrival of death. First, incipient putrefaction, indicated by the peeling off of the cuticle and the exhalation of an acid odour. Secondly, relaxation of the joints and muscles after the body has become rigid. And, lastly, the test of electrical galvanism. The body sometimes retains its warmth after death for twenty-four hours; but, in the majority of cases, the limbs become cold long before death takes place. Sub-vital action often occurs after death. Digestion has been known to continue. The tissues which possess the least vitality during life, such as the hair and nails, sometimes grow for a considerable period; and coffins, showing many inexplicable phenomena of this nature, have been opened. Twitch- ings of the face days after death, due to rigidity, have frequently given a false alarm. Buried bodies are sometimes found half out of their coffins and lying in all attitudes. In cases of cholera it is common to discover the body turned face downwards weeks after burial. These things are not evidences of entombment alive, but are physical effects of rigidity. Corpse-physiology is not yet understood; but it may be taken there is much to be told that is as yet undreamt of.

Thought, emotion, and the power of willing, which make up the consciousness and mental nature of man, are inseparably bound with the brain and nervous system. After the dissolution of the body and the thinking organs can thought go on? If man is a machine first, an animal afterwards, and a conscious being next, why should not all be but a "quintessence of dust"? But, if there is something more, to what bourne does it proceed? Where goes the life, or what remains of it when that which used it dies? Streets of gold and gates of pearl, or undying worm and fire unquenchable, may inspire the imagination of a Milton or a Dante to depict scenes of joy and beauty, or scenes of appalling misery—white- robed hosts "flinging down on the jasper pavement their crowns of amaranth and gold," or writhing wretches torn and rent with agony. But what are the realities, if any, which these figures symbolise? Scripture is designedly silent. Paul is caught up into a third heaven, whether in the body or out of the body he cannot tell, and the words that he hears are "unspeakable words, which it is not lawful for a man to utter." Lazarus comes forth from his rock-bound sepulchre; but the secrets which he could reveal are buried forever in the eternal silence. What we know not now we may know hereafter.

9

CORPSES AND FUNERALS

Slumbering Celebrities—Not "Obit" but "Emigravit" —Exposing Corpses— Strange Returns—Funeral Customs: Ancient and Modern—Death an Evil and a Joy—Lares and Penates—"Gathered to their Fathers" —Mummies and Hieroglyphics—The Sacred Beetle— "Book of the Dead"—Cremation.

The various ideas as to what becomes of people when they throw off the mortal state have a singular family likeness. Thus the belief in slumbering heroes—not dead, but sleeping—is common in mythology. There were always some who escaped the common lot of mortality, and were withdrawn awhile from the world to return as champions of race and country. Everyone knows that, according to folk-lore, King Arthur is still sleeping in the plains of Avalon, watched by three queens. Longfellow has made familiar to us Hiawatha, for whose return the Red Indians are even now watching. The Emperor Barbarossa is alive somewhere in the heart of a Thuringian hill, dozing till his head shall grow through the table before him and reach his feet, when he will awake and re-appear. In a cellar beneath the Castle of Krom- berg, Holger Danske, the Danish hero, slumbers, waking for a few minutes every Christmas Eve, on which occasion an angel visits him to relate how matters prosper in his native land. The Portuguese, for centuries after the battle of Alcazar in 1578, looked for the re-appearance of their King Sebastian, whom they obstinately refused to believe was slain by the Moors on the field. Thomas the Rhymer is, in the imagination of some Scottish peasants, yet dwelling in fairyland. Wordsworth only versifies a current rural superstition in "Lucy Gray," the child who disappeared mysteriously, but was still believed to be living.

Popular tradition has always been loth to realise the grim fact of death. The spirit which inscribed, not "Obit," but "Emigravit," on the tomb of the great artist of Nuremberg, runs through all these legends of sleeping heroes. When a reigning monarch or a successful usurper had succeeded in removing some inconvenient claimant to the throne, he usually found it a harder task to convince the populace that his rival was really defunct than it had been to send him to the world of shadows. Loyal Yorkists long doubted if Richard III. had been actually slain at Bosworth Field. Henry VII. found it difficult to assure his subjects that the sons of Edward IV. really perished in the Tower. The common custom of exposing to view the corpse of any celebrated person whose decease was convenient to the ruling powers—a practice still continued, chiefly in the cases of Popes and Monarchs—was an effort to combat this popular contumacy. The histories of the long line of pretenders who personated royal and famous characters show how readily the populace caught at the idea of escape from death. A substitution may have taken place on the scaffold, as is alleged in the case of Charles I., or in the prison or coffin. The person might still be living in fairyland, or in Paradise, or in a distant country, according to plebiscitary fancy. In this way the religious tale of the Seven Sleepers has been credited by the devout of all ages. There is the story of the sleeping beauty among the oldest of our nursery narratives. Again, the romance of the enchanted damsel, the lady of the Sparrowhawk who waited for the bold knight whose kiss should break the spell that bound her, half inclined Sir John Mande- ville to undertake the quest himself. In the "Bridal of Triermain" Scott has versified a similar phantasy, where the heroine is aroused from a magic sleep of 500 years' duration. Did not the "Great Twin Brethren" appear at the battle of Lake Regillus, and gain a victory for Rome? St. James is credited by devout Spaniards with charging at the head of the chivalry of Castille, mounted on a white horse, at one of Cortez's battles in Mexico. Southey poetises the legend which sets forth how "Five Friars Minarites," who had promised Queen Araaca to say a mass for her upon the day of her death, re-appeared some time after their martyrdom by the Moors and fulfilled their pledge by officiating at the altar in her chapel while she lay expiring. Probably the belief in these strange returns from unknown realms was strengthened in former ages by the extraordinary reappearances which often took place in actual life. Men might disappear for half a century, and then return from a foreign dungeon, a scarcely known country, or a desolate region "beyond seas." But what shall we say of the embodied ghosts or spirits of the nineteenth century?

Superstition in regard to the disposal of the dead is not less pregnant with weird fancy. It is much more likely that the element of fear, rather than the element of love, was the characteristic emotion of the earliest nations where corpses were concerned. As the ghosts of deceased persons and the totems or the material spirits of all things were supposed to exercise a malign influence, propitiation by sacrifice and the like was the order of the day. Almost all nations have regarded death as an evil; but the historian Strabo describes a race of people, living in one of the districts of Mount Caucasus, who mourned over the birth of their children and celebrated their funerals with rejoicing. Such an instinct, however, is not consonant with the average promptings of nature. Accordingly it is found that, as civilisation advances, funeral rites are typical of some sort of love and the hope of future life. The rudest method of disposal of corpses is that of the nomadic tribes. They simply expose the bodies, leaving them, in many cases, where they expired. Some tribes, like the ancient Ich- thyophagi, throw their dead into the sea, and think that thus they have got rid of the ghost which otherwise might haunt them. The Wanyamwesi leave the defunct to be devoured by the beasts, and other peoples keep dogs and animals for consuming the corpses. It is strange that among the Parsees, who are a most cultured nation, the custom of exposure should also continue. They bring their dead to round monuments, called Towers of Silence or Dokhmas, to be eaten by vultures, who take up their quarters in the structure. The Scythians, or some of them, eat their dead—a practice which is usual among cannibal races Burial in holes, caves, temples, or out-of-the-way places, is an improvement on the simple abandonment of the body. The Moors pile thorns on the corpse to keep off the beasts. Some tribes build the bodies in the walls of the dwellings; others suspend them till they rot and fall away. A number of American tribes bury their children in the wayside that their souls may enter into passers by. Cremation is an old practice—perhaps among the first. Variations of it were found in embalming the bodies for the purpose of quick destruction, and drying them on trees and artificial scaffolds before burial. The position of the body in the grave has often been a matter of superstitious importance. We find that some bury their dead in a lying posture, others in a sitting attitude. Some bodies, again, are laid east and west—a suggestion, no doubt, of solar symbolism in connection with sunrise, the reputed home of deity, or sunset, the reputed region of the dead.

In progressive ages many of the funeral ceremonies are suggested by the notion that death is a journey of the soul from this world to some invisible other. The belief in object-souls is mainly responsible for the burying of meat, drink, weapons, horses, money, servants, etc., with the corpse. Just as a man had a soul, so his food, his horse, etc., had souls, which souls attended the deceased soul when he was dead. The soul of the warrior rode on the soul of his horse, and used the soul of his weapon. Laplanders lay a flint and steel with the corpse to light the dark journey to the other sphere. Greeks put an obolus in the corpse's mouth, to pay Charon; and the ignorant Irish place a coin on the lips to meet the reckoning at purgatory. Many have buried treasure to buy salvation for the deceased; and Catholic priests now-a-days say "masses for the soul" for a consideration. Sacrifices of animals, wives, slaves, for the spiritual use of the departed in the next world, have been usual. The Arab leaves the dead man's camel to die on his grave. The Hindoo suttee, or sacrifice of the wives, is well known; and the Fijian, acting on the same idea, resorts to strangulation, instead of sanctified combustion. Chinese have a curious practice of flying paper images over the grave; and the Russians put a paper passport into the hands of the corpse as a testimonial of virtue, to be shown to St. Peter at the gate of heaven. The fear of ghosts has led to peculiar precautions among some. Greenlanders take the body out of the window or a hole in the side walls to confuse the ghost; and the modern Egyptians turn the body round, so as to make the ghost giddy, that it may not know its way back.

The Greeks and Romans either buried or burned their dead, and their mourning was symbolised by periodical feasts, image-heirlooms, preservation of relics as instruments of human power, and worship of the manes or souls which were supposed to preside over graveyards and funeral monuments. It is said that the worship of the Lares and Penates arose from the custom of burying the dead in the houses, owing to the belief that the spirits hovered about for the protection of the inhabitants. The Jews kissed the dying person and covered the face, it being no longer lawful to see it. When the coffin was lowered into the grave the relatives were the first to throw earth upon it. Jeremiah, who mentions the "mourning women," shows us that hired weepers and bearers were common at Jewish funerals; and Maimonides says that the poorest Jew was obliged to hire two players on the flute for the burying of his wife. Josephus informs us that, at the burial of Jews of distinction, the burning of perfumes and spices was very common; and the Talmud states that 80lbs of spice were consumed at the funeral of Rabbi Gamaliel. After the crucifixion Nicodemus brought to the body of Christ 100lbs of myrrh and aloes; and the custom of the Jews in perfuming the sepulchres of the dead led to the practice adopted by the Greeks of anointing tombs and monuments. The sepulchres in which Jews were "gathered to their fathers" were somewhat similar to the catacombs in Italy, excepting that the entrance was so narrow as to be shut by a stone. There was a distinction generally understood between affliction of the heart and lamentation as an affair of the nerves. "Professional" grief took the form of "renting" the garments with a knife, cutting off the hair, wearing sackcloth, and throwing dust upon their hearts to remind them that "dust we are, and unto dust we shall return." The tombs were periodically whitened for cleansing purposes, and it is to this custom that the allusion is made when the scribes, pharisees, and hypocrites are compared to whitened sepulchres.

Like the Egyptians, the Jews and Greeks embalmed their dead; but the practice was never characteristic, as in the case of the former people. We learn from Herodotus and Diodorus Siculus that the relations of deceased Egyptians smeared their faces with clay. When the corpse was brought to the embalmers, models of mummies, highly finished and painted on wood, were exhibited for the selection of the friends. It was believed that the soul remained with the body while it retained sufficient soundness to preserve the divine essence, and the solemnity of embalming was confided to the priesthood. There were three main modes of embalming, varying in excellence according to cost. A typical system was to extract the brains with instruments through the nostrils; then, from an incision in the side, to extract the contents of the abdomen, the cavity being washed with palm-wine and filled with a resinous substance mingled with myrrh, cassia, and the most odoriferous spices. The body was then sewn up and steeped in nitre for ninety days, and Belzoni says that heat was used to draw off moisture. It was then bandaged with cloth, saturated with gum, and swathed from head to foot with about 200 yards of covering five inches wide, upon which hieroglyphics, stating the titles, dignities, and other matters relating to the deceased, were inscribed. Sometimes a beetle, which implied regeneration, and an idol symbolical of faith, were placed on the body. It was then placed in a sort of plaster receptacle or coffin, richly embellished with hieratic and other writings, and deposited in a sarcophagus similarly adorned. The modern Egyptians, Sonnini and Groff mention, simply press all impurities out of the body, stop up the pores and apertures, and perfume it all over. It is then buried beneath a little pillar or head of stone, terminated by a sculptured turban. It is disputed by some that embalming had any reference to a belief in the resurrection. The judgment of the dead before burial is a peculiar piece of Paganism. Forty-two judges sat and heard charges before the body was interred, refusing burial in cases where the accusation was grave. The recent researches in Egyptology have thrown much light upon the funeral ritual, and M. Maspero, a member of the French Archaeological Mission in Cairo, has shown, in the *Revue de l'Histoire des Religions,* that the puzzling "Book of the Dead" is but a guide to the infernal regions, containing prayers and spells to protect the soul from a crowd of fabulous monsters—an interpretation corroborated by the new papyrus discovered at Thebes. Mohammedan rites have borrowed much in the way of formality from the Jews and Egyptians. The faithful were placed in the coffin sidewise on the day of death, in order that their faces might look towards Mecca, and the gloomy procession rushed along as fast as possible to the cemeteries.

Most modern customs are more or less exact representations of the ancient native practices. Cremation, after either the German or Italian pattern, appears, however, to increase in popularity. The tendency is to dispense with all *de mortuis* triviality and surviving superstitions; and that is well.

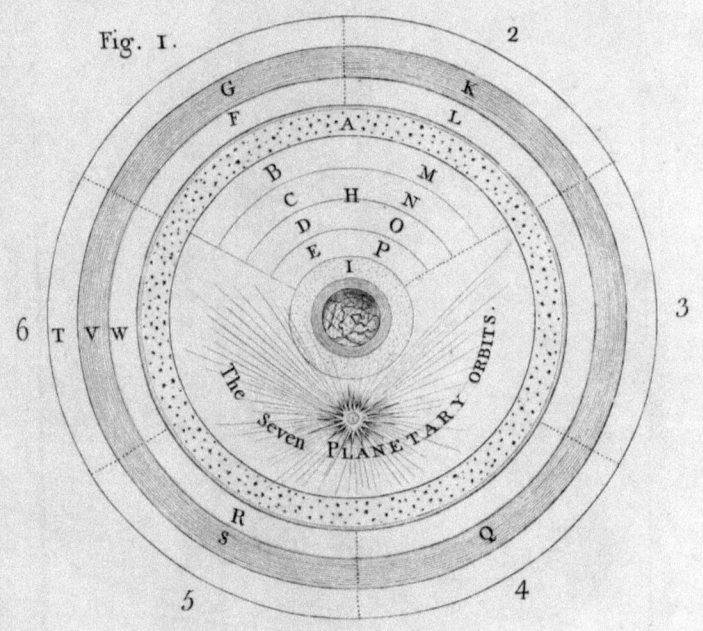

10

OCCULT FORCES: ANIMAL MAGNETISM, ETHER, AND MESMERISM

Electrical Monomania — "Earth-currents" — Electric Odds and Ends—Magic and Magnetism— The Theory of Molecular Vortices or Vortex-atoms—Artificial and Natural Magnets—Is Matter Motion? —Ether—Schopenhauer—Fourth Dimension Space—Spirit Marvels —Animal Magnetism—Astral Light and Fluid Aura —The Nerves and the Vital Principle—Ancient Electro-Massage — The "Evil Eye" and Arts of Fascination"—Movement Cure—Demon-possession and Star- craft— Ode Force — Vril —Braidism — Table-turning and Thought-reading—Willing—Muscle Study—Protylic and Dynaspheric Forces— Keely's Motor—Moral Polarisation—The Godward Impulse—Auto-suggestion and Hypnotism—Fashion in Physic—Psycho-therapeutics and Electro-therapeutics — Sleep — "Malades Imaginaires"—Mesmeric "Passes"— Localised Electrisation—Electropathic Apparatus— Women's Ailments — Neurasthenia—Emotional Miseries—Rites at Secret Societies—The Law of Inhibition—Hypnotism Physiologically Considered—Is it Catalepsy? —The Occult in Theosophy and Spiritualism.

It may be a matter of controversy whether Prometheus or Franklin first drew electricity from the clouds; but there can be no doubt that the new force has other duties than to disestablish gas and rob steam of its occupation. Gradually penetrating all the sanctities and secrecies of life, and keeping society in a constant state of unnatural excitement, electrical science would seem to be inducing a new form of monomania, destructive alike of healthy citizenship and domestic happiness. Had it been confined to telegraph wires, electrotyping vats, and dynamo machines, its natural functions might have continued their exercise without obloquy. But it has been dragged into all sorts of services and enterprises. First, it was offered to humanity as a curative agent. Somebody pointed out that people could obtain the benefit of certain invigorating "earth-currents" by simply sleeping with the head to the north and the feet to the south. Then beds were insulated from the floor with pieces of glass for the purpose of curing rheumatism. Pocket batteries and plates for the removal of nervous and other affections soon followed in great variety. There was something to put at the nape of the neck; something to hold in the hand; and, between the two, you got a tingling sensation. The "electric ring" was a mere circle of copper, with a bit of zinc inserted: and, together with the electric comb, electric jewels, the electric toothbrush, the electric garter, and the electric knife-sharpener, and for that matter "electric sugar," apparatuses were provided which nearly answered all the ordinary duties of defective existence. The scientific *gommeux* then began to wear breast pins containing death's head moths, or gibbering skulls, which could be set into motion by electricity, manufactured in the waistcoat pocket. A match became too common to light the gas with, so burners were started with the patent electric illuminator that is warranted not to explode, and is much too big to be taken as a poison. Ventosus, Aquafluens, and the Vaporifier have been deposed by this insidious motor, and it looks as if coal accounts and gas bills would be permanently eliminated from the miseries of the taxpayer. We may yet be awakened by a current which cooks the breakfast while the dressing process is proceeding, and the trouble of letter-writing and visiting may be done away with when everybody will be in telephonic and phonogramic communication with everybody else. The burglar will find himself paralysed the moment he tries a back door or unfastened window, and evildoers will be disarmed by induction coil instead of by truncheon—nay, even the removal of murderers and the slaughtering of beasts, which is much the same thing, will be effected by strokes as sudden and painless as that which felled the impious King of Rome at the altar of Jupiter. Life may be thought worth living in the *regime* of the *dolce far niente*, especially when its production can be controlled without Malthusian assistance, and the reversal of the principle of the conservation of energy clears away the obstacles to perpetual motion.

When the curiosity of the ancients was baffled, they resorted to such things as divination and sorcery. The magician was the scientific man, and the mysteries of his art were inseparable from those of religion and philosophy. We have changed all that now. Science is the opponent of the supernatural, and all explanations of mystery which are not consonant to its canons are stigmatised as pure charlatanism. The savant shows that the correspondences between the universe—planets, worlds, animals, and spirits—are mainly phenomena of electricity; the modern wonder-worker amends and revives ancient arts of starcraft, dream, face and palm reading. The "sacred art"—whether black or white— of antiquity was quackery; the supernatural science which has taken its place claims a religious character, for it seeks the moral influence of matter over mind, or of mind over matter.

What magic was in the thaumaturgy of the past, magnetism is in that of the present. The question thus arises, What is magnetism? Everyone knows that matter is composed of molecules or ultimate particles. Ampere has shown that around each of these molecules, or a portion of them in substances which are capable of magnetism, there circulates a current—that is, there is certain motion acting perpendicularly to the axes. This makes each molecule a small magnet. Clerk Maxwell and Sir William Thomson have enlarged upon this view and established the theory of Molecular Vortices or the Vortex-Atom, which is generally accepted. According to this explanation, all electrical phenomena are due to the existence of matter under certain conditions of motion or pressure, varieties of which are friction, contact, and chemical heat. Matter itself is only a particular phase of motion in the something called ether which fills up all space. The form of motion in the ether which makes matter is the vortex ring. The cells of that matter which is magnetic rotate or revolve hence in vortices. When the magnetism or electricity is brought into action the energy is supposed to exist, not in any alteration of the molecular magnets themselves, but in the bringing into line of their axes under an inducing influence. Thus, when a toy magnet draws to itself a pin, the axes of the molecules in the revolving vortices are all brought into line, and attraction ensues because these axes are in regular order. Before the inducing influence sets the force in action the magnetisms are combined round each molecule, and mutually neutralise each other. The inducing influence is a force greater than that of the mutual attractions of the magnetisms round the molecules, which accordingly become separated and arrange themselves in this regular position round the molecules, though they cannot be removed from them.

In nature there are found magnetic substances, such as the loadstone, which have the power of attracting iron and other metals. Besides these natural magnets there are *artificial* magnets, so called because they possess their power of attraction through being rubbed by a natural magnet. The force in magnets is distributed unequally, the greatest being at the ends. The two points where the attraction is the most powerful are called the poles, which have received the names of positive and negative, and the law of their action is: Poles of the same name repel each other, and poles of contrary name attract. To explain this an hypothesis, now exploded, was adopted to the effect that there were two magnetic fluids, one of which was called the north or boreal, and the other the south or austral, each of these acting repulsively on itself, but attracting the other. It was then found that there were substances containing the two magnetisms, such as iron, steel, cobalt, just like ordinary magnets, but differing in this, that the magnets held the two magnetisms in each molecule separate, while in the magnetic substances the magnetisms were combined, and the substance had no poles. When the magnet was placed in contact with the magnetic substance it separated the two magnetisms of the latter, and this is called magnetic induction. Thus it is possible to magnetise iron and steel.

But, while magnetism is manifested only in a small number of bodies, another force—electricity—can be produced in all. Unlike gravity, electricity is not inherent in bodies, but is evoked by a variety of causes, such as friction and heat, magnetism being among them. In 1819 Oersted showed that there was an identity in the causes which produce electricity and magnetism. Formerly there was a distinction between statical electricity, which was produced from friction, and dynamical or voltaic, which resulted from physical and chemical sources. But now these forms of the force are convertible. The different forms of electrical energy, as we know them, are that which is produced in a galvanic battery, where chemical affinity is transformed into electricity, that resulting from thermo-electric piles, where heat is directly converted into electricity, and work transformed into electricity in electro-dynamic machines, which are either magneto-electric or dynamo-electric.

In order to understand what is the producing cause of the motion of the molecules which leads up to these results, it will be necessary to consider what is meant by the ether. Aristotle added to the four elements, which were accepted in his time, another. This was called ether, and, being supposed to be eternal and unchangeable, it was considered the *primum mobile*, or source of all activity. It was a material substance of a subtle kind, imagined to exist in those parts of space which are apparently empty. Early learning invented ethers for all sorts of reasons: for planets to swim in, for constituting electrical and magnetic atmospheres, for conveying sensation from body to body, and for enabling specially- endowed persons to see what others could not see. Out of all these hypotheses the only "ether" which has survived is that invented by Huygens and Euler to explain the propagation of light. On this undulatory theory all bodies and spaces are filled by this subtle and elastic medium, which is named "luminiferous ether." The luminosity of a body is due to the rapid vibratory motion of its molecules which, when communicated to the ether, is propagated in all directions in the form of spherical waves; and this vibratory motion, being thus transmitted to the retina, calls forth the sensation of vision. Thus light is not itself a substance; and its medium (ether) is distinct from matter and air, and is all-penetrating. Hence, on account of its great tenacity, it is uninfluenced by gravitation, and, though it offers no appreciable resistance to the motion of the denser bodies, it is possible that it hinders the motion of the smaller comets like Encke's. There can be little doubt but that the inter-planetary and inter-stellar spaces are not empty, but are occupied by some such substance, which is the most extensive and uniform known. Its existence reveals an intimate relation between the phenomena of light, heat, and electricity. The ether is homogeneous or continuous in its physical constitution; though, so far as its motion is concerned, it is molecular. Now, some such molecular medium is required to explain electro-magnetic phenomena. If there is an ether associated with matter, we have a reason for the molecular vortices of static electricity; the kinetic or dynamic electricity is then simply the energy of the motion set up in the wires or other needful apparatus.

But the uses of this medium do not end here. It is stated by some to be an agent of inter-action between distant bodies, and to fulfil other physical functions. Thus it may constitute the material organism of beings exercising functions of life and motion as high or higher than ours are at present. Or it may affect the human constitution and framework in ways of which we know nothing.

Schopenhauer practically asserts that ether is *will*. The human will is the only thing, he states, which is known universally to be capable of changing motion. As matter is everywhere and in motion, there is a universal consciousness, and to this everything mystical is to be traced. After the same manner, Cardinal Newman founds an argument for the existence of God in his "Grammar of Assent." Will is the only designing thing; the world is a design; therefore, God is a conscious Being.

In 1829 Lobatschewski, speculating on the higher dimensions of space in connection with geometry, was led to assume a curvature in space. This implied the idea of what is termed the Fourth Dimension (used to explain certain marvels of Spiritualism), in connection with which ether is a most important consideration. Already we know three directions in which motion in space is possible. Take a square box, and you can move it in straight lines in three, and only three, different directions. Professors Clifford and Zollner suggested that there is possibly a Higher or Fourth Dimension in space. Suppose that space is capable of changing its shape; suppose that there are bends and twists and wrinkles in it. Then each bend or twist in the ether filling all space goes to constitute an atom of matter, and matter is simply made up of bends and twists in the ether. Hence, if space became even or smoothed of all its wrinkles, there could be no matter. Space, as we know it, is not capable of bending; thus the possibility of there being another or Fourth Dimension arises. Of this ampler space our space is but a section or portion, and a portion which is curved or circular. Accordingly, if we travel round it we find ourselves at the point whence we started. The Fourth Dimension, consequently, may be thus formulated: As the point is to the line, as the line is to the surface, as the surface is to the solid, so is the solid to the Fourth Dimension. Thus we are beings living on a plane or a small section of space. But beings living in the greater space of the Fourth Dimension have capacities unknown to us of the Third Dimension. For instance, Spiritualists who understand this theory will tell you that FourthDimensional beings or spirits will put an object into a closed box without passing through any of the sides, for to them a box is as open in the Fourth-Dimension space as a cup is to us in the third. Or changing the figure, a tall man will see over a higher wall than a tiny man. In this sense they deny that there is any occultism in spirit manifestations.

There have been many theories announced which claimed to have discovered some kind of magnetic force in living beings analagous to the action of the magnet on the metals. This influence is known as Animal Magnetism, and there are many variations of it—such as electro-biology, mesmerism, clairvoyance, astral light and fluid aura, odylic or odic force, and hypnotism. The belief is that there are some peculiar nervous conditions in which body and mind are influenced by a mysterious force from another person or a something. The mind depends on the brain. Too much or too little blood weakens the intellect. From the brain, owing to the promptings of the will, messages are carried along the nerves. The agent of this we do not know; but it is called the Vital Principle. When its force is diminished we sleep, and in sleep we store it up. It is assumed that the principle may be a condition of animal electricity, possibly resembling static electricity or Franklinism, generated perhaps by the friction of the blood against the arteries. Thus electrical currents can be aroused in the human body.

The priests in some of the nations of antiquity threw persons into what is now known as the hypnotic sleep. In this condition the mediums commonly uttered prophecies. Aryan Cyneticus mentions a sort of electromassage used in the treatment of dogs and horses in 234 A. D. The Romans applied the same system for the improvement of the human form. The early Chinese, the Greeks, and the

Egyptians and Arabs had a vague conception of animal magnetism. Touching for the evil was a sort of recognition of bodily electricity, and the Swedish movement cure suggested its existence. The "evil eye" and the arts of "fascination" to this day are made accountable for the withering of trees and destruction of crops; and the modern Greek has not a more abiding dread of the ** ****** than his ancestor had of the *******; while the *mal occhio* of Italy of to-day is not a more prominent article of the peasant's creed than was the *fascinatio* among the legendaries of Pompey and Caesar and the m*alus oculus*. Greatrakes and Irish scrofula curer followed the magnetic ideas of Swedenborg. Gassner, a Catholic priest, held that the majority of diseases were the result of demoniacal possession, and were to be cured through exorcism and by the electricity of the nervous system. Mesmer declared that the stars exercised an influence on the human body, and that magnetism would cure disease, because there was an occult force permeating the universe and affecting the nervous system. In 1845 Baron von Reichenbach announced a new "imponderable" or "influence, " developed by certain crystals, magnets, the body associated with heat, chemical action, and electricity. This he called *Odyl*, *Ode*, or *Odylic* force, and the idea of the existence of some such mystic power affects even now many scientific minds. Braid, the celebrated Manchester surgeon, first formulated the mesmeric and kindred states in *Neurypnology* (1843). He rejects all theories of supernatural influence; denies the presence of a "magnetic fluid, " and maintains that hypnotic and ordinary sleep are analogous. His was a neuro-hypnotism or nervous sleep.

Most people have wondered at the mysterious qualities of vril as explained by Lytton,[1] and of many other inscrutable omnipotences related in romance. These fictions as to wondrous unseen forces are but correct transcripts of popular fancies. Thousands believe in a psychical force behind "table-turning," "thought-reading," and spirit trickery. It is no use to prove to them that half-a-dozen pairs of hands of persons who unanimously "will" and use pulsative pressure all in one direction, produces the motion of a table along the carpet. They cannot believe that Mr. Irving Bishop. Mr. Stuart Cumberland, *et hoc*, are simply muscle-readers, whose skill depends on the fact that hardly anyone, in thinking of a movement, is able entirely to suppress the tendency to carry it out. The dodges which the Psychical Society exposes, and the "spookism" which it substitutes in connection with spirits and the world of shadows, is typical of superstition in another direction Mr. Crookes's "protylic" force, which was possessed of inconceivable powers if rightly used, still retains votaries. The receipt for "inspiration," which Mr. Laurence Oliphant prescribed is peculiar in its way. This mystic lays it down that an "inter-atomic stuff," or "dynaspheric force," which is the medium of the transmission of ideas from one mind to another, explains all the phenomena of Hypnotism, Spiritualism, Telepathy, and Occultism generally. But—woe to his theory—he quotes the impossible motor of Mr. Keely, of Philadelphia, in which a force of 250 horse-power is developed by the vibrations of a tuning fork, as a proof of the power and potency of his noumenon.

There has now been a considerable advance upon Occultism in this character. Hypnotic moralisation, also called moral polarisation or electricity induced in unconsciousness, is the description given to the producing of moral states of mind upon persons asleep. This attempt to etherise the human creature claims to lead up to the religious idea: the capacity of man to receive spiritual impressions, or the nature and meaning of the Godward impulse. Pseudo-Theosophy of the Blavatsky type, with its unknown seventh cosmical element and supersensuous faculties, is an illicit and absurd *extravaganza* of an idea which might be turned to great advantage in scholarly hands. The suggestion of the theory is that some outside power, some element of determination, influences the will; that the mind, irrespective of our *will* or bodily organism, is put into direct mental connection with a stronger mind, for the time being, notwithstanding time, distance, and material obstacles. In evidence of this phenomena of hypnotism are adduced. A man is sent to sleep or into a state of semi-catalepsy either by the "suggestion" of the ordinary circumstance attending upon that condition, such as closed eyes, etc., or by wearying out the intellectual awakeness by having the medium concentrate his gaze and attention upon some bright object or other things. Everywhere the sole cause for the execution of a movement is the bare idea of the movement's execution. If the idea occurs to a mind empty of other ideas, the movement or object of the "suggestion" will infallibly take place. But, if additional ideas conflict with the idea of a particular action, these block, or "inhibit," as it is called, its performance. Thus, if we think of our little finger moving, and allow no other idea to interfere with this idea, in a minute the finger will alter its position. Even when other ideas are in the mind, the motion constantly takes place, though insensibly. By suggesting in a whisper, to a person who is dreaming, to dream such and such a dream, it is well known that the operator, if the medium's constitution admits of it, can compel certain actions to be performed and certain dreams to be dreamed. Now, when a person is thrown into an artificial or hypnotic dream the intellectual or psychomotor centres of the brain are cast into the background, while the reflex or automatic centres are called into activity and receive sensorial impressions, which become arrested before conversion into conscious ideas. On this account no memory of what has happened during the sleep remains. The medium first falls into torpor or dazedness, consciousness then disappears, and movements suggested by the operator are automatically continued. Absolute forgetfulness follows, and illusions and hallucinations may be produced which are purely subjective and without any external reality. This "treatment by suggestion" is being put to curative uses. It is rapidly becoming a fashion; for still there are superstitions in physic in some ways quite as curious as the preference shown centuries ago for one amulet over another, or the belief in the superior efficacy of moss scraped from the skulls of criminals over live toads tied to the soles of the feet. The method is to cause the hypnotised patient to concentrate his whole mind upon the part affected. Under this influence the vascularity, innervation, and function of the part is said to be regulated according to the locality of the disorder. Dr. Tuckey, in prophesying a great future for psychic medicine, warns us that, if such a "gift for healing" be allowed to fall into unworthy hands —owing to the powers which the operators would have over their fellow creatures, and especially women— it would be a national disgrace.

This idea of the penetration of the human body by ether and electricity has given rise to two prominent methods of medical treatment, the results of which are too important to be passed by. The one is psychotherapeutics, and the other electro-therapeutics. The former attaches some degree of belief to faith-healing, so far as the mind can influence the body. It is adopted especially on the continent, in some quarters for the relief of nervous and other diseases. Liebault remarks that ordinary sleep is a result of auto-suggestion—that is to say, we act on our own feelings, that we are fatigued, that we should go to bed, and that before sleep we should put the light out. He states that hallucinations and dreams are common attendants upon natural sleep, and, in some cases, remain after the sleeper's awakening, and are acted upon. If, then, patients should be hypnotised, they are capable, as in dreaming, of acting on suggestions made to them. Rubbing of affected parts and other treatment is resorted to, while the "faith" in the cure of the patient is induced. Of course, these operations are only additional to the ordinary anaesthetics; they are of use chiefly in affections of the brain, nerves, and digestion. The older school of medicine denounce treatment by suggestion as a delusion or a form of hysteria, induced only in impressionable women or in men of unusually feeble mental and physical organisation: or, as a means of healing, only useful for *malades imaginaires*, who are always in search of some new medical dissipation, or among the classes where the emotional and functional faculties have unusual predominance. The practitioners contend that every person who has not an inability to concentrate the mind is susceptible to the treatment. Nerve specialists are unable to explain how or why the hypnotised person is influenced to a cure. Magnetisers and mesmerists used to hold that, to influence the patient, the operator required to be in robust health, on account of the exhaustion of the processes both for mind and body. They strained, or seemed to strain, their will-power, and employed much muscular force in making "passes." But the modern school regard hypnotism as a simple result of psychical and physiological laws, and dispense with all the affected foolishness of their predecessors.

Electro-Therapeutics had for its father Duchenne who introduced the Electric-hand, which was a combination of electricity with massage and muscular manipulation, or medical dynamics, the current being passed through the body of the operator. The principle is that it assists paralytic rigidity, and preserves muscular motion by clearing the way for the action of the nerves without using drugs—stimulation being believed to increase the oxygenation of the blood and nutrition. Neuro-pathology relies mainly on this nerve vibration, accompanied with localised electralisation by the method of low and prolonged galvanic currents. Those who believe in it as a remedial system argue that electro- pathic batteries, chains, and bands worn on the person do not cause the current to circulate through the body; for it is sympathetically retained within its coverings. The result is that scars are produced on the skin from pressure, and no benefit to speak of ensues, As illustrative of the efficacy of prolonged and direct electralisation, Legros and Onimus electralised some puppies daily, and at the end of six weeks found those which had been so treated weighed more and had grown larger than others of the same litter. It is stated also that a tree with a continuous current through its roots will grow better than by natural means.

Organic diseases of the nervous system—the result of either the want or superfluity of nerve power— though common to both sexes, are especially frequent with women, owing to the intricate relation and sympathy between the nervous system and sexual function. Nearly half of the female sex suffer from neurasthenia, which is a purely nervous derangement, with an emotional element added. Every faculty becomes exalted, neuralgic pains are felt in most parts of the body, the senses are perverted, spasms and paroxysms become common, and anaesthesia or a diminution or complete loss of sensibility often occurs. The elastic muscular coating of the arteries contract sometimes to such a degree as to stop the flow of blood. Dr. Charcot, the renowned Parisian nerve doctor, who has produced all the hypnotic effects upon hysterical patients, declares that this irritable defectiveness may account tor the sword blows which were given to the Convulsionaires without causing bleeding. In such people there is generally excessive emotional excitability, unchecked by voluntary efforts, and a craving for sympathy while they refuse it to others. This morbid craving prompts them to exaggerate a real illness, or feign it— even to inflict bodily injury to arouse compassion and attention— and throws a useful light upon cases of genuine fanaticism. Recently a case occurred in London in which a lady was being attended at the same time by five doctors. She fancied she had something the matter with her heart, her liver, her nerves, her eyes, and insisted on a specialist being told off to attend to each particular organ. Needless to say, she still lives, notwithstanding the doctors. Emotional irregularity is very odd. In many secret societies the mystical initiation is intended as a sort of nervous terrorism. The surroundings are made awful and weird. The candidates are told they must submit to be bled, to be "gutted," and the like. The rites are realistically gone through, dreadful oaths sworn, and, as the subjects are blind-folded, a very great effect is produced on nervous and sensitive natures.

The fancies of the mesmerists urged Dr. Carpenter and other physiologists to study more closely the reflex action of the ganglia at the base of the brain and the cerebrum. It was concluded that the symptoms of hypnotism were connected with the sensorium, which is that portion of the brain which receives impulses from the nerves coming from the organs of sense, eye, ear, nose, skin, and so on. Professor Huxley discovered that mesmerism might be artificially produced in persons who had received an injury to the brain, and he instances the case of a man who had received a bullet wound behaving sometimes in a purely automatic way without consciousness, and sometimes perfectly intelligently. Neurologists declare that impressions upon the senses may be made without the person having any consciousness of them. In the hypnotised state our consciousness is thrown out of gear, and we make the movements, without knowing it, which are conveyed to our senses. If we were awake, we should simply imitate the movements of the operator with a perfect knowledge that we were doing so. But sensory impressions are made on our eyes (the hypnotiser never performs from the back), and those nervous and muscular mechanisms which lead to unconscious imitation are aroused. The medium becomes an automaton, and the operator performs upon him through the sensory nerves. Thus he is in the state of a somnambulist who acts the movements of a disturbed dream; but his hypnotic sleep is not so profound. The patient is made to gaze on an object until fatigue is induced; various "passes" or movements are gone through by the operator of no use except to make the thing imposing; the ideas become irregular; the pupil of the eye dilates, because, as Heidenhain explains, of *inhibition*—that is to say, the restraint of the nervous action. Hence one set of recipient or sensory cells in the brain's intellectual side are brought into a state of exalted irritability by the preliminary operations; the part concerned with voluntary or conscious movement are inhibited or prevented from performing their natural functions; voluntary action is interrupted, and hypnotic movements depending on the impressions made upon the senses of the patient are performed involuntarily. Not long ago M. de Meyer showed how hypnotised persons were insensible to pain by cutting and beating them while in the sleep.

Most people cannot be hypnotised, because their presence of mind or power of self-control is too strong to permit of the bodily energies being paralysed by the sensory impressions adopted by the operator, or because their power of concentrating their attention upon what the operator suggests to them to do at the outstart, in order to fatigue and deaden their consciousness, cannot continue for the few minutes necessary. Those who have been hypnotised once can be readily hypnotised again; but the time of the operation is usually about fifteen minutes. Hysterical and excitable people, with a dash of superstition, are easily hypnotised, and medical science is proving the close connection of hypnotism with disease, especially in those—chiefly women—who suffer from hysterio-epilepsy. It may interest some to state the physiological theory which covers every case of hypnotism. It is as follows: —The cause of the phenomena lies in the inhibition or restraint of the activity of the ganglion cells of the cerebral cortex—inhibition being brought about by gentle, prolonged stimulation of the face, or of the auditory or optic nerves. Some sensation must be communicated to the patient, or else he will not move. He is insensible to pain, like persons in fits, owing to disorders of the nervous regularity. The rigidity or catalepsy of the muscles in the hypnotised person is easily explained by the ordinary laws of reflex action. Accordingly, hypnotism is but a natural or induced nervous disease—artificial catalepsy, useful sometimes as a substitute for chloroform and in the treatment of the insane, the somnambulistic, and the morbidly excited.

Thus animal magnetism is a peculiar physiological condition, excited by the perverted action of certain parts of the cerebral nervous organs, and not caused by any occult force. Ether is the all-pervading force which modern mystery-mongers make responsible for their gate- money quackeries. There is a market for such wares, and a large market too. Crazes and fashionable fads are decidedly on the increase, and the trades of the Spiritualist, the clairvoyant, and the fortune-teller are apparently by no means unprofitable. Theosophy, as it is improperly called, is the latest of the claimants upon popular credulity. An Asiatic creed, filled with beautiful traditions and imagery, and possessed also in some respects of a high moral code, is emasculated of the grossest superstitions, many of which are foisted upon the weaker-minded sections of civilised communities' as the only true creed. Savants have carefully studied the growth of Buddhism and described everything worth knowing about it, just as they have dealt with Mohammedanism or Confucianism. But, notwithstanding their efforts, in an Asiatic monastery, inaccessible to the European, where the secrets of nature have long since been revealed to the faithful, Mahatmas of infinite antiquity, and possessed of incredible power, only await the approach of true believers to teach them unutterable things. To facilitate matters, a Russian lady and an American gentleman have been chosen to show the old faith with a new face in India and in Europe, and act as the interpreters of the Mahatmas, who play extraordinary pranks with nature and its laws. Meanwhile communications are received and given in all sorts of strange ways, and the esoteric Buddhist is gradually elevated to the seventh heaven of ecstatic credulity. Yet these poor Theosophists are, to all appearances, sane people, and are, no doubt, sincerely shocked at the gullibility of the Neapolitans with their childish belief in the liquefaction of St. Januarius's blood. Spiritualism is but a more vulgar form of the same delusion. But it is surely very remarkable that numbers of educated people should be confessed Spiritualists at this time of the day; still more remarkable that many of them should be, as Robert Owen was, thorough Materialists. No amount of detected imposture seems to shake the confidence of those who believe in peculiar communications from beyond the tomb, which are so oddly conveyed through articles of furniture. Spiritualists of the highest culture will sit for hours in a darkened room awaiting some not very clever conjuring trick, and look upon writing on a slate with reverence little short of that which they would feel for a veritable writing on the wall. In most ages some of the ablest thinkers of the time—not excluding men of science as well as the most complete Atheists—had a rooted belief in mystical influences external to matter, which they could not pretend to account for or reduce to any law. But such cases are more or less the result of congenital influence and association, or characteristic of the tendency to take for granted that which would be looked upon as very slovenly in any really scientific consideration. When Bailly, Lavoisier, and Franklin examined into the Mesmer trickery, they went to work in a proper fashion. But to-day those who have undertaken the task of investigating the pretended possession of occult powers leave the laws of evidence on the threshold of the inquiry, and, accordingly, a hankering for mysteries is a prominent note of the time.

---

1. *Vide* "The Coming Race."

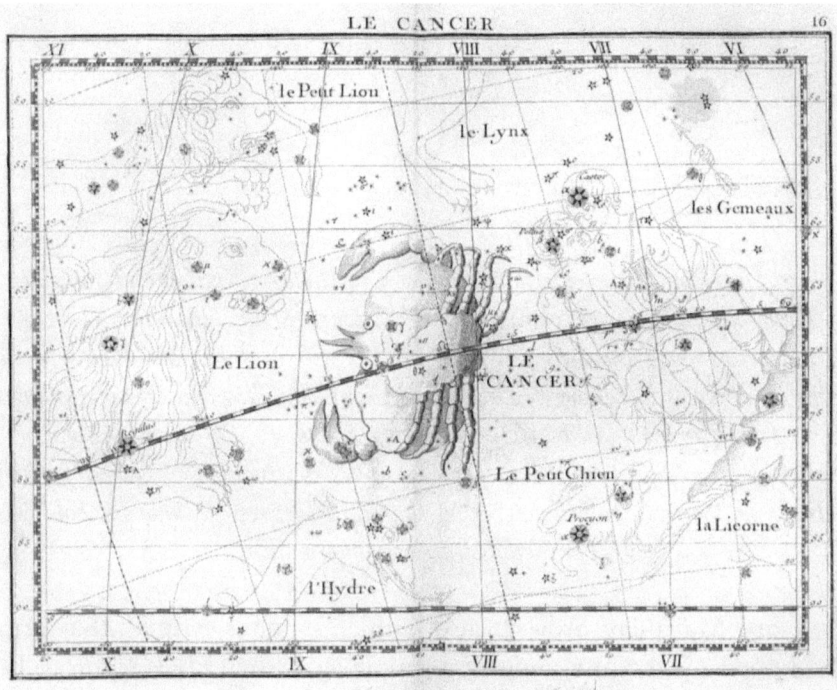

11

ASTROLOGY AND ALCHEMY

Superstitious Fireworks—Hermetic Sciences—Astrology: Natural and Judicial—Phallism—The System of Emanations—Houses of the Heavens—Hermes Trismegestus and Paracelsus—"Holy Water"—Elixir of Life and Philosopher's Stone—Phlogistic Theory —Divination—Fortune-telling and Dream-reading — Palmistry—Ordeal by Bible and Key—Dreams— Psychism—Origin of Spiritualism—"Spirit-circles"— Doctrine of Re-incarnation—Mystic Toys and Tricks— "Soirees Fantastiques"—Mechanical Marvels—"Cunni Diaboli"—The New Science of Abnormalism.

Lord Macaulay proved, by arguments unanswerable, that great poetry is the utterance of a simple age, when life is vigorous but uncomplicated, and the minds of men are not perplexed by abstract ideas. The antique bards, whose work has been the admiration of all succeeding time, had the instincts of children with the strength of heroes, and he who would rival them in a latter day must escape from the bonds of knowledge. "He must take to pieces the whole wit of his mind and become a little child"—observant, credulous, passionate, thrilling with the wonders of existence which he does not even try to understand. The same considerations apply to early superstitions. Many notions of primitive man were inaccurate, of course; but it does not follow that he was always wrong, or that we are always right in the interpretation of physical phenomena. With his mind full of ghost ideas, and as the life of his fellows left them in the form of breath, and escaped to the atmosphere, the groves—anywhere, it was natural that his worship, which was a result of fear, should extend from sky to earth.

Why it was nobody can say—perhaps because its colour was like that of the sun—the primitive man's successor connected gold with the principle of life and the essence of those intermediate powers—the demons or spirits—so wonderfully defined by Plato. According to the interpreters of nature—and when a superstition is once launched it is very hard to make it lose its footing—each person was put under the charge of a particular planet, which ruled the destinies and acted as a godfather, who might be held responsible for all misdeeds. When those destined to be personages in after life were born, Nature was supposed to oblige with a great display of fireworks —meteors, shooting stars, comets, and luminous appearances generally, so that everyone might recognise the coming man from birth, and know to whom to give the lollypops of the period. Extremely bad men rarely died of disease, but were removed from the scene of their sins by a convenient thunderbolt. Earthquakes swallowed up indecent cities, and summary justice was executed on a smaller scale by yawning chasms of a size to suit the order, taking in a whole band of conspirators or a select family party, as the case might be. Nature also used to keep in touch with the human race by means of the animal creation. Doves spoke oracles, and flocks of geese indicated augurs. When the bold baron was pierced by Paynim lance in distant Palestine, three black crows would be sent flying over his ancestral castle to warn his lady to provide her mourning paraphernalia; and when a treacherous visitor insinuated himself into the domestic circle, a raven, perched on the chimney pots, croaked till the visitor was ejected.

In numberless other ways did Nature show her sympathy with mankind; but she no longer does so in the old fashion. We still get shooting stars; but when we look in the morning paper to see who is born, we only find "The wife of Jones Robinson, Esq., London, of a son." There still are thunderbolts; but they never strike down, entitled "black sheep," or even the leading politician on the other side, whose cup of evil we pronounce to be full every morning in the train. There are no chasms provided for Boards of Works, Directors' Meetings, or Squire Justices; and the Stock Exchange stands as securely as St. Paul's itself. No comet comes to warn us of the outbreak of chicken-pox, and when the income tax is raised never a raven croaks.

It is disheartening work to kill by analysis the romance and sentiment of the less learned ages. The oriental mind delighted in marvellous extensions of the material surroundings of life, rather than in the finer and more intellectual phantasies of the West. But in both types of imagination there is much to admire as well as much to excite disgust. Notwithstanding the grossness and sensuality from which they arose, astrology and alchemy, which may be called the Hermetic Sciences, were the forerunners of our natural philosophy. From them Copernicus deduced astronomy; Toricelli and Pascal weighed the atmosphere, which achievement was the foundation of physics; and Lavoisier discovered oxygen, thus destroying all ideas in regard to elixirs and omnipotent essences.

Beginning in India, the Black Art stated the problems which are for the most part yet unsolved. Astrology preceded alchemy because it required only powers of observation. The nations of antiquity believed that the heavenly bodies were the instruments which the gods used to regulate the course of events in the world. This moral influence was regarded in two ways. Natural astrology simply predicted the motions of the sun, moon, and stars. On the other hand, judicial astrology concerned itself with the influence of the constellations on man and empires. It was a practical superstition founded on false philosophy. The influence of Phallism—the worship of the generative powers of the sun and of mankind—asserts itself largely. It was supposed that the procreative principle of nature acted by pre-established laws, and not by the varying impulses of the human will. As all creation came from the Divine impulse, and all things were of the one substance differently fashioned, it was only needful to find out in what mode the celestial bodies operated at the moment of birth to discover what would happen to an individual afterwards. This was the System of Emanations, which has played an important part in superstition; for, since plants, animals, and everything else emanated or proceeded from the deity, the observation of the motion of objects in nature made possible such miracles as prophecying and fortune-telling.

The first star-gazers had no knowledge of optics, and they did not know that the blue of the heavens is a mental appearance, caused by light traversing our atmosphere before it strikes the optic nerve. Many of them worshipped the stars themselves as the gods, just as the ignorant now-a-days worship the idol instead of that of which it is a symbol. It was thought that spots were marked out on the earth for temples and towns, and that malignity could be shown to animals and plants. Heraclitus, "the Obscure," went so far as to declare that truth was mixed up with the atmosphere that the wise might breathe it. To the early imagination the sun was a torch, and the stars candles. Else it was fancied that the universe was like an egg, the spots on the shell representing the constellations, or like a huge animal of the highest organism. The Egyptians peopled the zodiac, or that path in the heavens about which the sun wandered with genii under the forms of rams, bulls, fishes, etc. The whole heavens were divided into twelve equal parts, or *houses*, which were represented in various fanciful ways, and named life, riches, brethren, parents, children, health, marriage, death, religion, dignities, friends, enemies. These were contained in the calendars and ephemerides, in misshapen hieroglyphics and rude notches, marking the days and their associations. The days of the week were each placed under the protection of some stellar deity, and by means of its signs the priests regulated the life of the nation. Thus Tuesdays and Wednesdays among the Arabs were the days for blood-letting, because Mars was the god of iron and blood. Plants, animals, minerals, countries, all fell under different planets, which exercised sway according to their place in the *House* of the Heavens. Mars, for instance, in the House of Death, meant wars, etc. This certainty of fate had a great influence on those religious systems—such as the Catholic Church—where the doctrine of Predestination had a place. If a man could not alter his fate, no responsibility was attached to him. Hence astrology became modified, and it was said that the stars only *inclined*, not *compelled*. This left the human will free, and conveniently explained any mistakes in predictions.

The two beliefs upon which alchemy is founded were borrowed from the East. The Persians insisted on astrology—the correspondences between the heavenly bodies and the human frame. The Hindoos declared that sinful souls peregrinated through the animal, vegetable, and even mineral worlds till they were absorbed into Deity or Moncti. Hermes Trismegestus—the originator of occult science—taught how everything, even heaven and hell, are of earth, that the supernatural was simply the natural, and hence all secrets could be discovered. The quest of all investigation, then, was the affinities between all things. The sun presided over the generation of gold, the moon represented silver, and Venus stood for copper and other metals. All things being related, there was some common element which could create them. In the laboratory only the moral quintessence and revelation of religion was to be found out. Thus grains of wheat (Haeffer shows), from the power in their carbon properties of resuscitating and reviving dead and calcined metals, were the symbols of the resurrection and of life eternal. Zosimus, the Theban, called mercury "holy water," and assigned it sacred functions. Alchemy, in the opinion of Geber, was the "Science of the Key," and Rhaze denominated it the "Astrology of the Lower World."

There were many methods of robbing the universe of its secrets. The rival systems of Paracelsus and Illu- minato Postel were the most important. The former argued that the universe could best be known by its *signatures*[1] In the eyes of all the alchemists, except Boehme (who, anticipating Hegel, imagined it a tree, and accounted for monstrosities as the offspring of diseased metals), the universe was a living organism. The latter contended that the first step was to obtain by tincture or projection solid or liquid gold—the cure of all evils, and thus to surpass material and rational nature. It was needful, Calid states, before engaging in any operation of alchemy, to consult the stars; for every body, by its form and motion, indicated its soul and natural properties. For centuries systems of search and experiment were hopefully but vainly relied on. The *elixir vitae* and the *lapis philosophorum* eluded all effort.

The philosopher's stone was regarded as a red-powder possessing a peculiar smell, and in those cases where it was alleged to have transmuted the baser metals into the all-powerful essence an amalgam of gold was employed to deceive the ignorant. The thaumaturgists of the Middle Ages in no whit advanced on their predecessors. Albertus

Magnus, *alias* Albert Groot, revived the theory of Geber, and speaks of universal affinity. Raymond Sully mixed his magic with allegories and invocations to Christ. Paracelsus, or, to give him his full name, Phillipus Aureolus Theophrastus Bombastus Paracelsus, superseder of Celsus, who always carried a staff with a knob supposed to contain either a demon or specimens of each of the elemental spirits—Robold, Salamander, Undine, and Sylph—which he was supposed to have bound to his service by magical spells, was perhaps the most important hermetic. He introduced the cabalistic theory of "astral light," and made some important chemical discoveries. Nostradamus, a supposed miracle-worker, and Stahl, the last of the dreamers, developed the Phlogistic theory (now refuted) that there was a separate element of pure fire (phlogiston) fixed in combustible bodies as distinguished from fire in action or burning.

The various superstitions which astrology and alchemy have suggested are of more modern interest than the root-sources themselves. Divination is an art or science, or what you please, which obtains in all times. Narrowly speaking, it means the obtaining of knowledge in regard to secret or future things by revelation from signs, oracles, or omens, through the medium of a soothsayer, who is either inspired, specially skilled, or in communication with Divine quarters. In his treatise, "De Divi- natione," Cicero shows that classic theology includes all sorts of revelations and divers arts, such as augury and astrology. Divination is usually considered as artificial and natural. In the former division haruspication or the consultation of the entrails of sacrificed beasts, prodigies, augury or the drawing of omens from natural phenomena, the spilling of wine, lots, hearing strange noises, meeting a hare, fox, or pregnant bitch, and astrology, found places. Foretelling by the flight of birds or the falling of lots did not necessarily depend upon intervening deities or demons, while the religious or second class took note of dreams and prophetic oracles which were supposed to be revelations made by spiritual insight.

Artificial divination rests upon association of ideas in cases of mistaken analogy and. symbolism. A tree planted at birth by withering or flourishing was a suggestive sign. Sortilege, or lot-casting, was done in Agamemnon's leather cap, and dice or astragali or hucklebones were frequently made for the purpose. Cartomancy, or fortune-telling, by means of playing cards, is still common; and, as in ancient times, we know that the two colours, red and black, resemble the two equinoxes, the four suits answer to the four seasons, the twelve court cards answer to the twelve months of the year as represented in the zodiac, the fifty-two cards equal the number of weeks in the year, and so on.

Dreaming for texts or verses of poets is also a very old pastime. Scapulinancy, or the divining by the cracks and lines in the shoulder blade, known in England, according to Bland, as "reading the speal bone," depended on imaginary symbolic associations. This sort of analogy is pretty well understood by those who know anything about palmistry, or divining by the lines of the hand, which, at the present day, has considerable influence with weak-minded young women and men. The art is supplemented by chirognomancy and other nonsense, which indicate their dictum by considering the hair, eye, elbow, chin, or nose. It seems, according to modern teaching, that there are five different sorts of hands—the Idealistic (delicate, with long and pointed fingers), the Realistic (short and square fingers), the Energetic (with spatulated fingers), the Philosophic (rough and knotted in the points), Mixed (with all or some of the peculiarities named). The left hand is always chosen for the augury, because the heart and brain are supposed to influence it most. The ball of the thumb is called the Mount of Venus, and the hollow of the hand the Plain of Mars. Lines of life, death, fortune, love, and so on, are calculated from the length and direction of the grooves in the skin of the palm.

Before the days of Pythagoras palmistry had its adherents, and it is curious to reflect what an altered world this would be were the rules of life which it would lay down for every infant born—except a casual Miss Biffen, who, having no hands, and consequently no palms, would have to be left to pursue her path unguided—to be followed. At the beginning of the study a question arises: Why should the hand be influenced by seven planets—the sun and moon, Jupiter, Saturn, Mercury, Mars, and Venus? The ancients knew only of seven; the moderns know of more. Why is it that Vesta, Ceres, Pallas, and Juno are omitted? And, again, it is accepted among the professors of the game that, according to the development of the various "mounts" and "lines," the qualities indicated by the planets are to be detected.

Stars, spots, circles, crosses, and other marks on the different mounts mean a great many things, not, of course, to be escaped. If a man has a star on the Mount of Saturn, he will be hanged. It is no good for the jury to recommend him to mercy, and for the judge to say that the recommendation shall be forwarded to the proper quarter. His doom is sealed.

Of course, such sillinesses as these are not to be confounded with physiognomy or face-reading—an art which everyone of us practises without knowing anything at all about the works of Baptista Porta and Lavater.

Another class of these arts depends on the unconscious or half-conscious action of some person, often the diviner himself. The divining rod, in which otherwise sane people believe, is supposed, when held in the hand, to dip in order to indicate a hidden spring of water or vein of ore, or a buried treasure. The ancient art of Cosci- nomancy recommended the suspension of a sieve, which gave its omens by the manner of turning. Similar to this is the ordeal by *Bible and Key*—the book being suspended by the key, supported by four fingers of the suspected person. Dreams have not only been considered as visits from ghosts, but often as supernatural signs to be interpreted symbolically; and among ancient nations Oneiromancy was a powerful instrument of politics.

In Sibly's "Occult Sciences" the rules are given by which the ancients and moderns read the horoscope of the newly-born. Romance and history are full of examples of predicted destiny. The astrologers practised chiromancy and other arts. They were excellent physiognomists, and, being wise over their fellow citizens in most other respects, they could cast a nativity with wonderful shrewdness. At the birth of Louis XVI., Villefranche was placed behind a curtain to horoscope the destiny of the future autocrat. Charles V. and Francis I. both employed astrologers to fight their battles. Beza believed that the star appearing in 1573 predicted the second coming of Christ. Richelieu secured Gaffarel, a Cabalist, as a member of his Council. Le Maister held that comets were means of divine justice; and both Napoleon and Wallenstein had ardent faith in their stars. The poet Dryden calculated the horoscope of his son, it is said, successfully. The idea of Reynaud, that the souls of men passed at death to the stars, is a metempsychosis surviving from religious astrology; and it is to star-craft that we owe the theories about heaven-sent rulers, "the right divine," and inspired prophecies.

In our own century fortune-tellers are still important personages. Endowed with the prophetic mantle, they consider themselves cruelly used when summoned before the magistrate for extorting money from the deluded victims. The passion for penetrating into futurity prevailed only a few decades ago alarmingly. That the notion is not by any means obsolete is evident from the many thousands of "Zadkiel's Almanack" and similar publications which are yearly sold. Indeed, as Mr. Tylor remarks in his "Primitive Culture," by the "modern period to which astrology remained an honoured branch of philosophy, it may claim the highest rank among the occult sciences." It is easy enough to understand why it should prevail in ages when animative intelligences were supposed to reside in the celestial bodies, and hence to admit that a child born under a certain planet was supposed to have corresponding characteristics. But why it has not met the fate of alchemy is strange.

Psychism in all its forms is only an elaboration of the ancient astrology. The general idea is that those effects which can be produced in the physical world, and are inexplicable by the known laws of nature, are to be considered spiritual. Elsewhere[2] it has been shown that all genuine phenomena of Spiritualism are scientifically explainable. But, notwithstanding this, thousands believe in the modern spirit movement, which was begun by Mr. and Mrs. Fox, of America, in 1848. A daughter of this couple discovered that strange knockings which disturbed the household were produced by an unseen intelligence, which would rap as requested—later discovered to be the spirit of a murdered pedlar. Thus began the science of communication with lost relatives and deceased persons. Kate Fox and her sister, who afterwards confessed their fraud, became the first "mediums" between the living and the dead. One rap was agreed upon to mean "no," three "yes;" and complicated rappngs symbolised letters of the alphabet. "Spirit circles" were formed, and Jackson Davis, another veracious American, wrote a work on "Nature's Divine Revelations," which was said to have been dictated in a clairvoyant trance. Home and other Americans turned an honest penny by practising the art. In 1855 a Spiritualistic religious movement animated the Yorkshire mind, and in other parts of England phenomena alleged to be produced otherwise than through the brain or muscles of the "mediums," such as furniture-moving, ringing of bells, thought-reading, floating of musical instruments and ethereal beings, quasi-human voices, "materialisation" of deceased persons, mesmerism, psychography (or spirit writing and drawing), spirit photography, solids passing through solids in a Fourth Dimension space, table-tilting, trance-speaking, medium "possession" by deceased souls, and divining rods, astonished a credulous public.

In France Allan Kardec promulgated the doctrine of re-incarnation, which taught us that our egos or souls were successively re-incarnated after intervals of spirit life. All the white magic of history was revived through the influence of the new movement. The optical tricks of Hippolytus were practised, and Roger Bacon's "Discovery of Miracles" ransacked for new deceptions. In 1863 John Maskelyne invented a cabinet in which persons vanished and were made to reappear by means of a mirror. Tobin and Pepper used the same principle in their "Cabinet of Proteus" at the Polytechnic, and Stodare in his illusions of "The Sphinx." Robin and others produced ghosts by reflecting a lime-lighted object placed beneath the front of the stage. Others rivalled the brazen head of Pope Sylvester II., which answered questions; the speaking figure of Descartes, the philosopher, who called it his daughter Franchina; and the wooden figure with a speaking trumpet in its mouth, through which a priest answered questions, exhibited by Irson before Charles II. The toy bird of De Wildalle which fluttered and warbled, the automaton flute-player of Vaucan, Maskelyne's two automata—"Fanfare" playing a cornet and "Labial" playing a euphonium, the written questions enclosed in sealed envelopes of Alexander the magician, the spirit tricks of Anderson "the Wizard of the North," the clairvoyance of Pinetti, the electrical illusions of Dobler, the *soirees fantastiques* of Houdin at his "Temple of Magic" in Paris, the dodges of ethereal suspension, the mechanical chessplayer of Baron Kempelen, the roping and sack feats of the Davenport brothers, the "Psycho" and "Zoe" of Maskelyne and Cooke—all found believers and improvers in Spiritualistic circles. No amount of exposure seems to be able to destroy popular belief in marvels which are stated or insinuated to be the work of spirits.

We study the religious books of the Buddhists, Brahmans, and Mohammedans. We collect the vaticinations of Delphi, Dodona, Ammon, and the like. We examine the book of Mormon and the visions of Swedenborg.

We notice modern revivals, and visit the meetings of Quakers and Peculiar People. We consult the almanacs of Moore and Zadkiel, and smile at the Apocalyptic romances which continue the cabalistic calculations of Pythagoras, whose doctrine was that everything in the universe was represented and governed by certain figures or numbers, to which he ascribed mysterious virtues We attend mesmeric and spiritual *seances*, and pore over the imaginings of Jewish seers, the writings of Christian saints, and every other effusion which professes to be a revelation from Deity or the Devil. We collate all these, and find that, though opposed to each other in detail, they agree in claiming some occultism. Sometimes the supernatural power is said to be imparted by the parent of the medium, himself supernatural;[3] sometimes it runs in the family, as "second sight" in Scotland; sometimes it comes on with fits, as among the Sybils and Pythonesses of old and the Dancing Dervishes of to-day. Sometimes, and especially in the East, it is an appanage of insanity; for none are so replete with visions and direct communications from cloudland as the religious monomaniac of the Swedenborg type. Sometimes the power descends through schools and colleges, and the mystagogue is initiated to wield the prong of the devil's tail as easily as the Old One amuses himself with pitching those who do not pay the priest hush-money from a bed of burning brimstone to another of eternal ice. Sometimes prophetic ecstasy was the yielding to the guidance of imagination and renouncing common sense, which was corporeal, in order to give the celestial faculties and the soul liberty. Hence the disordered wanderings of a mind out of order are often taken for supernatural perceptions. Sometimes forefuturing was produced by the intoxicating exhalations from cun*ni diaboli*, or those fissures in the earth which were the sensual symbol of the female organs, as at Delphi; or, as the human soul was considered an emanation of Deity, it was thought possible, among Mahatmaites and others, to cultivate or develop oneself to the functions of seership. There are signs that the supernatural itself is undergoing an "avatar." Under the name of "Abnormalism," a new philosophy of the mystic is growing in favour. Its sphere is the sphere of unconsciousness and those things which lie outside of and seem to defy the laws with which we are acquainted; to deny the existence of which is, according to Schopenhauer, not "scepticism, but ignorance."

---

1. See "Faith-Healing and Medicine."
2. See chapter on "Occult Forces."
3. "The Prophecy," in The Lady of the Lake.

12

SPECTRAL ILLUSIONS, GHOSTS, AND SECOND-SIGHT

Natural Hallucinations—The Eye—12,544 Facets—Am- I-not-to-believe-my-own-eyes— What's the Price of Potatoes? —Ghosts: Human and Animal— British Legends —The Death Coach—Spectre-dogs—"Padfoot"— The Werewolf Myth—Household Shadows—Causes of Supernatural Sight-seeing—"Second-sight"—"Wraiths " and "Fetches"—Strange Cases of Seeing— The Reasons Why.

Apparitions, spectres, or ghosts have been reduced by the scientific to the vulgar level of a mental delusion, caused by some species of disease in the organs which affect the vision. But scattered survivals of the primitive belief in ghosts and ancestor worship still linger on, in spite of the rapid advance of modern culture. The mysteries of Theosophy, Re-incarnation, Spiritualism, and the like, are but "new departures" in a very antique superstition, which mistook natural hallucinations for the supernatural, through a jumbling up and confusion of the human senses. It is not wonderful, when we consider the eye, which is the principal organ in the seeing of apparitions, either optical or mental, that many people have believed the grave gave up its dead, and that other violations of the natural law were supposedly frequent.

Sight diminishes in power as man develops and civilises. The savage has the advantage of the civilised man; the lower animals the advantage of the savage. The eagle enjoys sight in excess; the earthworm is totally deprived of it. Insects are richly endowed with seeing power. The little whirlwig *(gyrinas natator)* which skims on the surface of standing water has a double set of optics—the upper portion fitted for seeing in the air, and the lower for seeing in the water. Spiders have from six to eight eyes, centipedes twenty, while the eyes of many insects (bees, butterflies, etc.) are composed of a number of facets, each eye being, in fact, a cluster of eyes. Dr. Hook counted 14,000 of these facets in the eye of a dragon fly, and Leenwenhock 12,544 in that of another. The latter naturalist adapted one of the eyes, so as to be able to see objects through it by means of a microscope. Puget discovered that fleas' eyes diminish as well as multiply objects.

These facts warrant us in believing that the human sight is capable of strange things when out of gear. The Am- I-not-to-believe-my-own-eyes theory is responsible for many a ghost. Daudet, in his novel of "Sappho," speaks of a Dutchman who sailed every sea, and who, when asked to describe what he saw, replied: "Guess the price of potatoes at Melbourne." In every country the solitary fact that struck him was the price of potatoes. How few can see well, even in healthy times, with both eyes! Most travellers who have written have earned the reputation of being ingenious perverters of truth and inventors of marvels. Some few have lied out of a desire for notoriety. But most, having neglected to use their eyes, were compelled to tax their memories for illustrations, and to draw upon their imaginations for facts. Partly to dislike of what is common, partly to the senses of colour and shape, partly to paralysis of the ophthalmic nerves, and partly to the commercial principle which urged Herr Kuyper, the Dutchman, to ask the price of potatoes at Melbourne, we have such prodigies as the sea serpent, the dragon, and the mermaid.

Apart altogether from genuine ghosts, what a museum of imaginary curiosities and monstrosities might be collected from the talk of travellers, but for the prosaic judgment enforced by railroad and steam. It was only the other week that the newspapers reported that a discovery had been made in Paraguay of a tribe of Indians with tails, stating that the type found had been photographed by a German in the interests of science. Doubtless many an embryo Darwinist pointed out the paragraph as an unanswerable argument against his antagonists. Vision unaided is often as delusive as untrained common sense. Not less important are overdrafts on the imagination than distortion of vision.

No particular time or place is assigned for the appearance of apparitions. The time is usually evening or night, and the place apart from the busy haunts of men. Ghosts frequently have appeared in human form; but it would seem that it is the rule rather than the exception for ghosts to take the form of animals. Possibly the primitive belief in the theory of metempsychosis—the transmigration of the soul from one animal body to another—made the doctrine of the animal ghost universal. And it should be known that Phallic significance is attached to the superstition which found origin in the early days, when animals were reverenced for their powers of propagation.

A long-standing legend informs us that at Beverley, in Yorkshire, the headless ghost of Sir Joceline Percy drives now and again four headless horses above its streets, passing over a particular house which was said to contain a certain chest with a hundred nails in it, one of which dropped out every year. In Shropshire, it is stated, a lady whose dead body had been robbed—she was buried in her jewels—walks in equine shape. Croker, in his "Fairy Legends of Ireland," speaks of the death coach, and quotes: —

> "A coach! But the coach has no head,
> And the horses are headless as it.
> Of the driver the same may be said,
> And the passengers inside who sit. "

A man who hanged himself at Broomfield, near Shrewsbury, is supposed to haunt the road between Yeaton and Baschurch as a headless black dog. It is not an uncommon belief that the spirits of wicked persons are punished by being doomed for a certain time to wear the shape of a dog. Mrs. Leathern, in her "Sussex Superstitions," mentions the fact that the spirit of a favourite dog is supposed to return occasionally to its terrestrial haunts. Traditions respecting these spectre dogs differ in various localities. In Devonshire they are known as the "Yeth Hounds," and are said to be disembodied souls of unbaptised infants. Wild Edric, a legendary hero, haunts the Stretton Hills in the form of a large black dog with fiery eyes. At Bagbury we are told of a very bad man, whose ghost was a roaring bull. Miss Burne, in her "Legends of Shropshire," tells us that the bull was captured, and, as he was compressible, he was shut up in a snuff box and deposited under Bagbury Bridge. In Cornwall, Mr. McHunt relates ("Popular Romances"), it is believed that, when a young woman who has loved not wisely but too well dies forsaken and broken-hearted, she comes back to haunt her deceiver in the form of a white hare. Wordsworth, in his poem entitled "White Doe of Rylstone," has embodied a Yorkshire tradition, which asserts how the lady founder of Bolton Abbey re-visited the ruins of the structure in the shape of a spotless white doe. The villages round Leeds have a nocturnal terror, locally called "Padfoot." The ghost is described as about the size of a donkey, with black shaggy hair, his chief amusement consisting in following the people by night.

The werewolf myth has prevailed in every European nation of Aryan descent. Gervase of Tilbury testifies that wolf-ghosts were common in his time; and Camden records that in Tipperary men were turned into wolves every year. Giraldis Cambrensis gives an older instance of the same superstition. Now and again the corpse would arise from its resting place in the form of a wolf; and even King John is said to have gone about as a werewolf after his death. On the west coast of Ireland the fishermen have a strong prejudice against killing seals, owing to a popular tradition that they enshrine "the souls of them that were drowned at the flood." According to a German piece of folk-lore, the soul takes the form of a snake—a notion which is shared by the Zulus and other Totem worshippers, who revere a certain kind of serpent as the ghost of their day. Another belief tells us that the soul occasionally escapes from the mouth in the shape of a snake, a red worm, a weazel, or a mouse—a superstition to which Goethe alludes in "Faust": —

"Ah! in the midst of her song
A red mousekin sprang out of her mouth.

We are told that Andaman Islanders held as a fixed belief that the dead vanished from the earth in the form of various animals and fishes; and in Guinea monkeys found in the locality of a graveyard are supposed to be animated by the spirits of the dead. In Mexico it was said that the souls of the brave were turned into beautiful singing birds; and some of the North American Indians believe that the spirits of their dead enter wild bears. Certain African tribes think that the souls of wicked men become jackals; and among the Abissoires, Mr. Tylor finds, there are certain little ducks which fly in flocks at night, being supposed to possess the souls of the defunct.

The ghosts with which we are most familiar are those of murdered or deceased persons. The shrouded forms and gusts of wind and slamming of doors are, of course, less interesting than such cases as we have quoted, and, accordingly, such subjects may be well left alone. It is quite possible for a person to speak the truth as to what he saw, and yet that no real apparition may have occurred. Almost every lunatic tells you what is seemingly present to his diseased perception, and most of the apparition cases have been connected with fanaticism in religious matters, owing to the mystery of what becomes of the soul after death. The majority of the poor creatures who subjected themselves in the early centuries of the Church to macerations and lacerations, and saw signs and visions, were simply persons of partially-deranged intellect. St. Theresa, who lay entranced for whole days, and who, in the fervour of devotion, imagined that she was frequently addressed by the voice of God, and that Christ, St. Peter, and St. Paul would often visit her solitude, was simply an example of a monomaniac. In these cases the eye may take a correct impression of external objects. But more is needed. A correct perception of the mind is necessary to a healthful vision. It is not only visual disease that gives rise to spectre-seeing. *Delirium tremens*, brought on by dissipation, fevers, inflammatory affections, epileptic attacks, hysteria, and disorders of the nervous system, upon which the senses and power of volition depend, are ready producers of spectral illusionment.

"Second-sight," in Gaelic termed *taisch*, is one of the varieties of spectral illusion or apparition; and attempts are being made to identify a resemblance between it and the *clairvoyance* of the animal magnetists. Second-sight has been defined as a singular faculty of seeing an otherwise invisible object without any previous means to that end used by the person who beholds it. It is a subjective power—originating, that is, in the mind or soul. It has formed the subject of a more regular profession than any other species of spectral frenzy. The power of the seer was generally regarded as an unaccountable accident of nature; but it could be obtained by anyone who would put his feet upon the foot of the seer at the moment of the ecstasy. The whole vision that was passing was then perceived by the novice, who, by putting his hand on the head of the other, and looking over the right shoulder, would remain ever after liable to a recurrence of the power. The seers, or taischers, as they were called in Scotland, generally lived solitary lives in wild regions, and the visions were chiefly of funerals, of strangers approaching the country, of persons drowning or falling in battle at a distance, and other subjects often of a mean or unimportant character. One peculiar case is related of a Monsieur Battineau, who held a situation under the French Government in Manuhur. This gentleman possessed the power[1] of foretelling the approach of vessels to land long before they were visible either to the eye or to a glass by the effect produced upon the atmosphere.

Suddenly, in the midst of some employment with or without company, perhaps the eyes of the seer would be visited with the supernatural spectacle at which he would gaze in astonishment; sometimes he would see a friend or neighbour with the appearance of a shroud around him; and, in proportion as the dismal garment rose high upon his person, so near was believed to be the approach of his death. Sometimes a boat would be seen with a party sinking in the waves, in which case intelligence of their having perished at sea was always expected to arrive soon afterwards. Occasionally the death of a friend was prognosticated by the sight of his coffin in preparation; but generally, when this was the object of the vision, a funeral company was observed, the chief mourners being perhaps hid from view in order to preserve a convenient obscurity as to the individual meant. These *wraiths*, or spectral appearances of persons about to die, were not confined to the Scotch; they were customary in Ireland under the name of *fetches*.

No less a person than Dr. Johnson was favourably impressed with the plausibility of second-sight. In his "Journey to the Hebrides" he relates that, in the course of his travels, he gave the subject full inquiry; but he confessed he never could "advance his curiosity to conviction, but came away at last only willing to believe." King James I., in his "Demonology," alludes believingly to the matter, and Sir Walter Scott went so far as to say that, "if force of evidence could authorise us to believe facts inconsistent with the general laws of nature, enough might be produced in favour of the existence of second-sight." Collins, in his ode on the "Popular Superstitions of the Highlands," declares that a seer in Skye foretold the execution of Charles I. at the moment his head was being severed. The execution of Mary Queen of Scots is traditionally stated to have been foreseen, and by many Highland seers. Dr. Ferrier, in his work on "Apparitions," gives personal corroboration of "seeing," though his opinion is adverse to the existence of the supernatural gift. Stewart, in his sketches on "The Highland Regiments," confirms instances which have occurred in his own family. Sir George Mackenzie, afterwards Lord Tarbat, communicated to Robert Boyle accounts of true manifestations, published in the correspondence of Samuel Pepys. Aubrey, too, the antiquary, in his "Theophilus Insu- larum," quotes about a hundred cases gathered from various sources, many of which are corroborated in Mr. Dalzell's "Darker Superstitions of Scotland." Thus there is no lack of competent authority to report on the matter.

It was generally allowed that, when a seer removed from his own country, he lost his power. But the gift was not peculiar to any people. Aulus Gellius relates that a priest at Padua beheld the last fatal battle of Pompey, which was taking place at Thessaly, and, at the close, exclaimed, "Caesar has conquered." The assassination of Domitian by his freed man, Stephanus, which took place at Rome, was seen by Appollonius Thyanseus at Ephesus, who declared before the crowd around him: "Well done, Stephanus; thou hast struck the murderer: he is slain." A maniac in Gascony is said to have exclaimed, "The admiral has fallen," at the moment when Coligny was killed in Paris in 1572. St. Ambrose fell into a comatose state while celebrating mass at Milan, and, on his recovery, asserted that he had been present at St. Martin's funeral at Tours, where it was afterwards declared that he had been seen.

But second-sight is by no means confined to times which are not modern. Curious traces are still found of it among savage tribes, and related as occurring in our own country from time to time. Captain Carver obtained not long ago from a Cree medicine man a correct prophecy of the arrival of a canoe with news the following day at noon; and, when Mr. Mason Brown was travelling with two *voyageurs* on the Coppermine River, he was met by Indians of the very band he was seeking, these having been despatched by their medicine man, who declared that he saw the travellers coming and "heard them talk." One of the most interesting instances of the so-called "second-sight" occurred in connection with the death of Mr. George Smith, the well-known Assyriologist. This scholar died at Aleppo on August 19th, 1876, about six o'clock in the afternoon. On the same day and about the same time, as Dr. Delitzsch—a fellow-worker of Mr. Smith's—was passing close to the house in which he had lived while in London, he suddenly heard his own name uttered in a most piercing cry. Dr. Delitzsch made a note of the hour and the fact, and some days afterwards the details of the death arrived.

When we recollect how history and tradition abound in examples of "second-sight," oftentimes apparently resting on evidence beyond impeachment, it is not surprising that the belief has had many adherents.

Believers in the theory base their faith, like most modern superstitions, not so much on metaphysical definitions as on the evidence of daily experience, it being immaterial to them how impossible a certain doctrine may seem provided it only has the testimony of actual witnesses in its favour. In spite of every argument combatting "second-sight," as against the laws of nature, it is urged that visions coinciding with real facts and events occurring at a distance—often thousands of miles away —have really been seen. It has, of course, been shrewdly remarked with reference to these predictions that the principle of "expectant attention" comes in. "Speak of the devil and he'll appear" is an example of those occurrences where we are carefully apprised of the instances in which they are justified by the event, while a studious silence is preserved respecting the infinitely more numerous instances of failure. It is believed by some that second sight is either the effect of imagination or of actual optical phenomena. When certain mental functions become diseased the sense of sight may indeed be imposed on by imaginary things supposed to be prophetic of future events. Idleness, solitude, ill health, and an imagination "intensely" diseased, coupled with the mother of all superstitions—ignorance—

may offer some explanation of these as of other mysteries. It is possible that a person brooding constantly over certain ideas would at length become suddenly possessed by a kind of waking dream, in which imagination pictured forth an occurrence formed out of the shreds of their habitual reflections. Such visions, if found to have shadowed forth actual occurrences, were coincidences— accidents. "Second-sight" can be explained in no other rational way.

---

1. *Vide Nautical Magazine, March, 1834.*

13

THEOLOGY AND THE 'ISMS'

"Robert Elsmerism"—"The Latest Decalogue"—Theological Conundrums —"Science of Religions"—Phall- ism, or the Worship of Sex and Sense—Solar Mytho- logy—The Linga and Yoni—Divine Trinities—AIale and Female Gods —Elohim and Jehovah—The Thera- peuts—Old Testament Plagiarisms—The Hindoo Chrishna—Only-begotten Sons and Virgin Mothers— The Atonement and Other Dogmas—Hot Cross Buns and Dyed Eggs—The Cross—Science and Supernaturalism.

What has come to be called "Robert Elsmerism," or religion free from dogma, is the best announcement of the attitude of modern thought to theology. It is a protest against the intolerance in matters of religion which would deny that there is another side to the moon. Walt Whitman revolted against rhyme, just as Wagner revolted against stereotyped melody, in search of a freer expression for the changing soul. So there is a protest against the *ipse dixit* of the shoddy sophistry which is relied on to bind together the vertebrae of orthodox Christianity. Those who know only the pulpit catchwords and chapel-echoes of their creed cry out for the retention of the form and the dogma as it is proved not to be. They cannot see that all the mysterious nonsenses, transcendental conundrums, empty abstractions, phantasmal creations, unknown elements, elaborate futilities, question-begging hypotheses, and pseudo- somatic somethings, which have gathered round the in vestigation of Being, Existence, Becoming, Final Cause,

Substance, Substratum, and so on, have been either unreal or suggestive of insoluble phantasies, and are now cremated in the limbo of erudite pretence. But there are others who are dissatisfied with the intellectual basis of a faith which is otherwise sympathetic to them morally and religiously. These do not base their belief upon any rational tradition, family caprice, or the personal proclivities of intellect, more or less weakly, nor upon schemes of life constructed upon subjective principles. They are disposed, under the influence of modern enlightenment, to seek a more rational basis for their faith. By a steady comparison of the whole, they find little difficulty in subscribing to "The Latest Decalogue": —

> "Thou shalt have one God only; who
> Would be at the expense of two?
> No graven images may be
> Worshipped, except the currency.
> Swear not at all; for, for thy curse
> Thine enemy is none the worse.
> At church on Sunday to attend
> Will serve to keep the world thy friend.
> Honour thy parents; that is, all
> From whom advancement may befall.
> Thou shalt not kill; but need'st not strive
> Officiously to keep alive.
> Do not adultery commit;
> Advantage rarely comes of it.
> Thou shalt not steal; an empty feat,
> When it is so lucrative to cheat.
> Bear not false witness; let the lie
> Have time on its own wings to fly.
> Thou shalt not covet, but tradition
> Approves all forms of competition. "

Christian dogmatics is usually divided into theology proper (existence of God), anthropology (man's creation, fall, and sin), soteriology (doctrine of salvation), escha- tology (judgment, resurrection, heaven, and hell), and ecclesiology (the Church and Sacraments). There are numerous sub-divisions, such as apologetics, exegesis, etc., more or less involved in a metaphysical Maelstrom and tricks of logical legerdemain. To consider all the subjects is sinful waste of time, and, accordingly, my method will be to survey theology with the object of showing how its mysteries are historically explained.

It is said in these days that there is no longer any theology. There is a "Science of Religions," if you like; but theology, as an exposition of the dogmas contained in Christianity, no. Oriental research, Biblical criticism, and subjective inquiry have destroyed the canonicity of the *acta* and the *logia*. The Gospels passed through half a century of oral tradition with the result that the written accounts of them present many differences and divergencies. Inherited creeds, which are the offspring of a widespread metaphysical disease, are remembered— from the point of view of scholarship— mainly as having failed to solve the problems of God, immortality, and duty. To-day we are no nearer the goal. It is felt that there is "something which makes for righteousness," an Inscrutable, a soul-hunger, an instinctive desire to worship, a godward impulse, and cults of the time invite us to console ourselves by reverencing, instead of the Hebrew God, nature, humanity, cosmic emotion, physical law, self, others, and universal happiness.

The forceps of criticism have brought to light strange analogies between the theologies of Paganism, classicism, and Christianity. That the roots of modern faiths are embedded in pre-historic notions is undoubted. The earliest expression of religion is found in the carved symbolism of a remote antiquity. When primitive man saw the universal operation of the reproductive forces by which organic life is propagated, he would naturally be awe-struck. The example of regenerative agency in his own person would be the first to strike him. He would then notice that, by the same principle, animals and plants were seen to be produced and multiplied. This mysterious power he was unable to define, and his feelings of reverence would induce him to seek some appropriate emblems. As, in our own day, pious devotees invest with sacredness memorials of heroes and events considered to have had a miraculous origin, so the savage would worship wondrously that which seemed to him to be the origin of his existence. It is not odd, then, that, in the monumental records of the oldest faiths—preceding the art of writing—actual representations of the reproductive (organs, in one form or other, for religious purposes, should be very prominent. In Europe, Asia, and America evidence of this abounds. The rough outlines of a phallus, or procreative member, sometimes in the form of a serpent coiled round a tree and sometimes round an egg, was frequently used as a memorial of the supreme act in nature. It is said, indeed, that these "finds" throw a glint of explanation on the story of Adam and Eve and the serpent in the Garden of Eden, on the "Song of Solomon," and other erotic romances which need not be mentioned.

But recognition of the creative principle was not confined to the human or animal being. The buds of spring, the blossoms of summer, and the ripe fruits of autumn were seen to be dependent on the impregnation of the earth by the sun. Hence arose an interest in the heavenly bodies; hence arose the sensual deities of Pagan and classic races, the classification of the signs of the zodiac, the impure rites, the celebration of the seasons, and of the passage of the earth through *personified* clusters of stars.

In this way solar mythology[1] originated. And we find that, even at the present moment, reverence for the sun and the celestial bodies has not ceased. In the altar architecture of India and of most European countries *lingatic* (male) and *yonic* (female) symbolism maintains an honoured place. Underlying many of the customs, ceremonies, and emblems which are known by more or less modern names, it is easy to detect the survivals of phallic worship. Though such symbolism is shocking to the ears of this age, it was otherwise to the ancients. Nothing natural could be, in their opinion, offensively obscene, and this circumstance is no proof whatever of depravity in their morals, but rather the reverse. Thus the point of all this learning which has been devoted to the Phallic and Arkite superstitions, and to trees and serpents, the Dionysiac or Priapic myths, sun and moon worship, goes to show that the earliest religion was a devout recognition of the male and female principles in nature in active combination. At first, primitive mankind were astonished at the creative powers of the *linga* or male symbol. In time the *yoni* or female symbol took its place in the worship of the Universal Reproductive Agency—the Unseen Power of Fecundation. It is, indeed, asserted by some that there was, in early times, a great religious war between those races which worshipped the male and those which worshipped the female symbol.

The adoration which was paid to the sun and the sky grew by easy stages into a worship of invisible persons or gods, among whom were the ghosts of the ancestors—all possessing fecundating powers. Of course, the sun-god or the creator would be regarded as the superior power, and the child-like faculties of early man conceiving the pains and miseries of life would soon evolve an evil deity, a destroyer who was in constant conflict with his colleague. In tribal life the prehistoric people usually reconciled their differences by the intervention of some third party, and this circumstance would duly suggest a Compromiser of the differences of the celestial belligerents. Accordingly, the idea of a Divine trinity found its place among the beliefs of mankind. The attributes which various myths ascribed to the deities would result usually in their being described by different titles. Thus we find the sun-god known as *Ormuzd* in Persia, *Baal* in Babylon, *El* among the Hebrews, and *Mithra* in India. The names of the same object would occasion confusion in the ancient mind, and, when we consider the numerous offspring of the deities and the ghost-souls of deceased chieftains, the plurality of gods, totems, angels, and devils, which constitutes Polytheism, is accounted for.

In the lapse of centuries the number and variety of the gods and the feasts and pageants held in their honour led to fierce disputes among the partisans of particular divinities as to their traditional origin. Priesthoods asserted themselves. Amid the wranglings many of the people, becoming sceptical in regard to their old faith, allied themselves to other superstitions. From this theological chaos Monotheism—the belief in one Supreme God—takes its birth. The belief in the Fatherhood of God was known thousands of years before the coming of Christ. Tertullian amusingly explains the strange contrasts between Christianity and the earlier Paganism by the fancy that the Devil, knowing beforehand of the ceremonies of Christianity, which was not yet established, inspired the Pagans to forestall the rites of the Gospel so as to rival and injure God. It would seem, however, to be beyond dispute that the God of the Bible is the direct descendant of the Sun- god worshipped as the chief fecundating principle in nature.

The Hindoo and Egyptian gods, distinct survivors of Solar and Phallic worship, were two-fold—male and female. In the first chapter of Genesis we read: "Let us make man in *our* image after *our* likeness......In the image of God created he him; *male and female created he them.*"

It was at Ur that Abraham, whose father was *Terah* ("a maker of images"), lived before he introduced into Palestine sun-worship for the planetary creed of the Chaldeans. He spent much of his time among *Yonic* devotees, and it may be safely concluded that he installed a form of Phallic worship and the Sun-god, El.

The works of Higgins, Richard Payne Knight, Drummond, Maine, Bryant, Tylor, Baissac, Dulaure, and many others, will give the conscientious Christian opportunity of contrasting his belief with facts. Myths were so borrowed and interchanged in primitive communities that misunderstanding of their meaning gave rise to new myths, and, being supposed to contain treasures of ancient mysterious wisdom, the learned persons explained them by further *mythical* expositions. M. Renan concludes, in "Le Pretre de Nemi," that it is impossible in regard to religious myths to get beyond the triple postulate—God, Justice, Immortality—or the idea of faith in the ultimate triumph of religious and moral progress, notwithstanding the frequent victories of folly and evil.

The savant recognises,[2] about 2000 B.C., the emergence of barbarian morality from the savage state under two types—the Aryan in Afghanistan, and the Semitic in Arabia. The nomad Semite, like all the ancient people in history, believed that he was living amid a supernatural environment. He imagined the world was governed by Elohim, by myriads of active beings, very analogous to the spirits of the savages. The spirits of Elohim were inseparable after a way, and without distinct proper names like the Aryan gods. Accordingly, the tent of the Semite patriarch—the primitive system of commune life in which one head was recognised as absolute—was the starting point of religious progress, and converted the world from Paganism, or the idea of many separate spirits, to Monotheism. Jahveh, the God of the

Jews, was adopted when national individualism impelled a people to *personify* the "spirit," the Jehovah of their race. At first a local and provincial deity, Jahveh—merely an ideal of divinity—became, through a sort of return to the old patriarchal Elohism, the Almighty Creator of heaven and earth. Jahveh soon becomes "the Just," as symbolical of the introduction of morality into religion.

Scholars have practically decided that the earlier stories of the Old Testament are of Indian antecedents. The Therapeuts taught Christianity long before Christ. Pantaenus, in the third century, went to India and brought back the Gospel writings alleged to be original. The present-day sects, who claim the purest Christianity, have been shown to cherish but the religious myths which once excited the emotions of the Egyptians, the Persians, and the Hindoos. It has been proved that the Creation, the Fall, the Deluge, the Garden of Eden, the ethics of the Ten Commandments, the miraculous narratives, the Ark of the Covenant, the Urim and Thummim, circumcision, the names of the patriarchs, the Sabbath, the incense, genuflexions, holy water, images' sweating blood, respect for relics, and rituals have all had their counter-parts in the worship of Osiris and Buddha. But, more important still, the keystones of theological controversy, the doctrines of the trinity and unity, the miraculous conception, divine incarnation, temptation by the devil, the cross, the crucifixion and justification, the atonement, hell, heaven, paradise, judgment, and resurrection, were common to the prominent religions thousands of years before Christianity. The connection and mythic meaning of all religions is no longer confused with the simple and universal elements which they all embody.

To understand Christianity, it is needful to know something about the mysterious and often disguised' resemblances in the symbolism of the world's religions. The study of the relations between existing faiths and those of the past shows us that every prominent dogma and ritual of the Christian Churches is but a modified reproduction of something acknowledged and practised by ancient nations. Professor de Gubernatis declares that, notwithstanding the beauty of Christian art and the fame of our civilisation, their basis has, till now, remained Pagan. The notion of the trinity which has prevailed widely can be traced to the relation between the male and the female principles of nature, and the vital product of both in combination. Divine trios existed thousands of years before Christ, and among them may be mentioned Brahma, Siva, and Vishna in India; Osiris, Isis, and Horus in Egypt; Odin, Freya and Thor in Sweden; the triple goddess Pussa in China; the sacred triads of Greece, Assyria, and Persia; and God the Father, God the Son, and the Bird or Spirit in the remote islands of the Pacific. Mr. George Smith, the Assyrian explorer, has reduced the claim as a supernatural revelation of the fable of Adam and Eve in Eden to a mere plagiarism from the phallic emblems—the forbidden tree and the wily serpent— familiar to the Israelites during their captivity among the sun-worshippers of Babylon. The Hindoo avatar, or re-appearance of deity in other forms, is the origin of the Divine incarnation in the case of Christ. In the mythology of India, Chrishna (Christ) is the son of Brahma (God), by Maya (Mary), a virgin mother, and usually called the "Saviour." He was born hundreds of years (600 B. C.) before the Christ of the Bible was heard of. He was bred among shepherds, and carried away shortly after his birth, lest a certain tyrant should take his life. The tyrant, hearing that he should be destroyed by the babe, ordered all new-born males to be massacred—a sculptured representation of which is to be seen on the rocks at Elephanta. Chrishna cured a leper and a woman, and washed the feet of the Brahmins. He descended to Hades, and at Mathura he is represented crucified before his ascent to heaven. He is pictured with a crown on his head, and stigmata on his hands and feet. Also with a hole in his side, and a combined *linga-yoni*, in the form of a crown, on his head.

There are many examples of immaculate conception. In Egypt Amun Othph is the offspring of the virgin, Queen Mautmes. Aesculapius, "the good Saviour," is the son of the virgin Coronis, and was found by goat-herds who were frightened at the fiery rays encircling his head—a sign of divine origin. Hercules descended from a human mother by the god Jupiter, and the offspring of Minerva were of virgin maternity.

Mithra, the Persian God, was known as the *Mediator*, as *Love*, and as the bringer of "The Word" from the Supreme lips. Champollion discovered, in the Temple of Dakkeh, sculptures of Thoth ascending to Heaven as the *Logos*. The atonement, or the propitiation offered by the death of the first-born son, was practised in India and Egypt, and the inhabitants of these countries were familiar with the doctrines of *justification*, *salvation*, and the *millennium*. The Madonna and child of the Christian had an early counterpart in Isis and Horus, or in Lakshmi nursing Vishnu, or in the Aurora and Memnon of Greece. The sacramental bread and wine and baptism were used in the mysteries of Dionysius. In Egypt, India, and China monkism was an institution. The hot cross buns of Good Friday and the dyed eggs of Pasch or Easter Sunday figured in the Chaldean rites. The "buns" were used in the time of Caecrops (1500 **B.C.**) in the worship of the goddess Astarte; but, instead of being marked with the cross, they were baked in shapes to imitate the *linga* and *yoni*.

The hieroglyphics of all early nations contain the cross. It is by no means the exclusive badge of the Christian faith. It decorates antique statuary and carvings. It was worn by females in Thibet and Japan as amulets. The gods of Greece had the cross as their sign, and the Phoenicians, Druids, and Hindoos built their temples after its model. In Mexico it was called the "tree of life." The serpent-images of the Chaldeans were common long before Moses raised one in the view of the people, and called it *memra*, the logos or word. The Crescent of the Turks, who still are worshippers of the female or *yonic* principle, carries us back to pre-Biblical days. In the *cross* we find the union of the male and female organs of reproduction. Its use was decreed as an ecclesiastical symbol at the Council of Nicaea A.D. 325 —one among many of the borrowings resulting from the contact of Christianity with Paganism when Constantine became a proselyte.

Little purpose would be served in detailing the various exposures for which the study of comparative religious mythology is responsible. Theology has resolved itself into the mere inquiry, Is it possible to reconcile Biblical teaching regarding man's creation, history, and destiny with the conclusions of scientific research? Geology has conclusively proved that the world, as it now exists, was not created out of nothing in the space of six natural days. Leading theologians are ready to compromise upon this matter, and to extend the doctrine of evolution to the Darwinian extreme, with the limitation that it may be true as applied to vegetable life and the brute creation, but that creation by natural law is not creation without God. They are willing to swear also that the Bible does teach that the Creator breathed the breath of life into the nostrils of man, and man alone, this being but condensed or symbolic history, and that man has fallen from a higher condition to a lower.

In regard to man's soul or immortality, science, of the Materialist hue, bases its argument upon the law of the inseparability of matter and energy in the world of un living or inorganic nature. Just as heat, electricity magnetism, and other physical energies can have no existence apart from matter, so the vital and mental energies are but peculiar rythmic motions in the molecules of matter. Thus man, dissolved into his constituent ammonia and carbon and lime, goes to enrich the earth and feed other generations of men. But, say the orthodox, to establish the possibility of future life it is only necessary to prove that spiritual consciousness and aspirations cannot be resolved into molecular motion. If matter is indestructible, if force is indestructible, why should not mind or soul be indestructible? It was Carlyle who said "it is unlike nature to spend seventy years in discipline and training and character to fling it away when complete, as a child flings away its plaything."

The restricted dogmatism of science, though it readily admits the sincerity of belief of most people in religion which depends upon supernatural or abstract powers, explains away the divine character of all forms of worship in a manner which cannot be ignored. The result of such analysis is to rob Scripture of its supernatural character, and to exhibit it as a development of the religious instinct in correspondence with the progress of national and individual life. Man, from the earliest times, in his ignorance, personified the forces of nature—sun, wind, and so on—and attributed what he could not understand to the power of an indwelling deity. Good or evil also were worshipped in concrete form as gods, and anthro- polatry, or the worship of deified or demoniac ancestors, grew naturally out of this primordial anthropomorphism, which prompted early mankind, and even such an advanced people as the Romans,[3] to imagine all power in the form of a human being, the mind being then unable to comprehend a force independent of an organic body. It is contended that an instinct towards higher things, or a yearning for the ideal—an exaltation which was more or less satisfied by the belief in God and the soul—

was translated by causes historical, physiological, and psychological, into the worship of Deity. Max Nordau explains pretty clearly the position of Scepticism in the matter. The longing, he says, expressed by man "for a higher intellectual growth, and an ideal for a consolation always ready at hand, for a powerful and mysterious protector in all emergencies, is no false pretension, but a genuine and ineradicable sentiment of religion. The continuation of early beliefs in the supernatural is an honest hereditary weakness." Concerning the Bible, the same author writes: "We know (from historical investigations) that, by this name, we designate a collection of writings as radically unlike in origin, character and contents as if the Nibelungen Lied, Mirabeau's speeches, Heine's love poems, and a manual of zoology had been printed and mixed up promiscuously, and then bound into one volume. We find collected in this book the superstitious beliefs of the ancient inhabitants of Palestine, with indistinct echoes of Indian and Persian fables, mistaken imitations of Egyptian theories and customs, historical chronicles as dry as they are unreliable, and miscellaneous poems, amatory, human, Jewish, and national, which are rarely distinguished by beauties of the highest order, but frequently by superfluity of expression, coarseness, bad taste, and genuine Oriental sensuality. As a literary monument, the Bible is of much later origin than the Vedas. As a work of literary value, to compare it seriously with the productions of Homer, Sophocles, Dante, Shakespeare, or Goethe would require a fanaticised mind that had entirely lost its power of judgment; its conception of the universe is childish, and its morality revolting. " This is a typical indictment, which may be taken for what it is worth.

"The net result of the whole negative attack on the Gospel has been to deepen the *moral* hold of Christianity on society, " is the weighty pronouncement of Mr. Frederic Harrison. Yet, notwithstanding this advantage, our Churches vulgarise their services; our congregations idolise their ministers, instead of their Maker; worship has become a sort of sensualism; dogma means offensive and unlettered contradiction; and the faithful neglect God. Theology attempts a feeble imitation of the mediaeval practice of applying scholastic philosophy to draw forth from the Scriptures the mystical truths of God upon which the revelation is supposed to be founded. And science—the pessimistic, the unsanctified—with its numerous shoddy adjuncts, such as bastard Theosophy and clairvoyance, alone is spiritualising religion, freeing doctrine from myth and mystery, widening the moral nature of the individual, and vitally coalescing God, natural law, and Christian morals into a rational theory of the universe.

---

1. See "Astrology and Alchemy" *supra*.
2. "History of the People of Israel."
3. *Cf.* Lares and Penates.

14

RELIGION AND RELIGIONS

*Fetish-Worship—The Taboo—330,000,000 Deities—The "Unmovable"—
Water-Oaths—Juggernaut and the Suttee—400,000,000 Worlds—The "Nic-
ban"—Taoism—Asgard and Valhalla—Easter—The Yule Log—Sacred Shams
—"Dynaspheric Force" and the Divine Feminine—Sects and Statistics—
4,000,000 Sermons a Year—Vital Religion.*

Systems of supernatural belief have sprung up like mushrooms. Each of these has been called a religion. They differed just according to the prevailing views of the nature of the unseen powers or Deity, and of the relations in which human creatures stood to them, to him, her, or it. There is no historical proof of the origin of religion, and hence it is needful to rely upon the theories and book theologies put forward from the time of Lucretius and the Bible to the present day.

The forms of philosophic and religious thought which claim a special insight into the constitution of Deity have been explained under "Theosophy." But more interesting still are the methods which different nations deemed desirable in the concrete worship of that which they fancied they understood. The collected monstrosities and puerilities shown at the Museum of Religion in Paris was a strange satire on the Godward impulse. On considering the display, the fact forces itself on the mind that exoteric worshippers are still, as ever, the most numerous, sentimental, and dogmatic—the blindest to the inner significance at the root of religion. Comparison of the oldest and newest faiths as they are contained in sacred books, monumental hieroglyphics, and rites; in the Chinese pagodas; in the sculptured images and mystic emblems of Indian temples; in the disentombed marble blocks of Babylon; in the stories of Bacchic orgies and Mithraic mysteries; in the sacred obelisks and paintings of Egypt; in the ruined shrines of the Druids; in the stony records of the Mexicans and others; in the coarse-nature worship and bloody sacrifices of Dahomey; in the Jewish synagogue, the Moslem mosque,, and the Christian cathedral, show the general identity which distinguishes the struggles and aspirations of humanity from the most primitive times to master the enigmas which beset our origin and destiny.

The impress of the greater manifestations of nature— its reproductive powers, its sun-light, moon-light, starlight, prismatic clouds, the storm-wave, the whirlwind, the pestilence—can be traced in the earliest religions. But this is the finer side of primitive fancy. Fetishism, the lowest existing form of reverence, is simply the superstitious reverence for any object in nature and art. It prevailed through Paganism; it survives to-day in Christianity. Asia, Africa, and the Oceanic Islands abound with such worship. In Whiddah a small insect, called the creeping leaf, is highly honoured. In Benin anybody can make whatever he likes his fetish or god— bones, egg-shell, clay, wife, anything. The Lacedemonians had a sacred stone, which, at the sound of a trumpet, was said to raise itself to the surface from the bottom of the river Eurotas. The ancient Germans and Gauls had their holy rocks, caves, trees, etc., which afforded miraculous aid; and at the present day in Ireland people afflicted crowd to a Catholic chapel at Knock, believing that, if they eat some of the mortar, they will be cured of their malady. In Iceland there was a stone which was supposed to have a spirit within. The Laplanders had a sacred mountain and a consulting drum. In some of the islands of the Pacific, if any person wishes to protect his property from robbery or trespass, he declares that it is *tabooed*, or placed under the guardianship of his gods, and, the belief that such is the case being universal, the property is safe from aggression. The West Indian negroes worship *Obeah*, or *Obi*, who was the same as the African *Ob*, against whom Moses warned the Israelites.

The Jews were continually inclining to idolatry. This is accounted for by their Elohistic beliefs and their several years of sojourn among the Egyptians, who worshipped sun and moon, and believed in lucky and unlucky days, dreams, omens, charms, and magic. Gods, to the Greeks and Romans, were only deified rulers and heroes, who had done something notorious on earth. In Greece the Hecatomb, or sacrifice of 100 animals at a time to appease the manes or restless spirits of the deceased, was a common occurrence. Atmospheric appearances were ominous of great public disasters; and long after the fall of the Roman empire Pope Calixtus II., on the taking of Constantinople by the Turks (1456) cursed and excommunicated a comet, and prayed, "Lord save us from the Devil, the Turk, and the comet," victory being claimed for his Holiness on the disappearance of the meteor.

In portions of Persia and India the Parsees, or fire-worshippers, called by the Mohammedans "Giaours" (infidels), still follow the faith of Zoroaster. He lived, according to Dr. Haug, 1,300 years before Christ, and inculcated Monotheism. God is the emblem of glory and light; hence the Parsee, when praying, stands before the fire or the sun as the most perfect symbol of the Almighty. The vulgar and the illiterate worship the flame as others do idols; but the cultured regard fire as an emblem. In tracing the religion of the Aryan or Indo-European race (which is said to have sprung from Iran or ancient Persia), to which we belong, this worship of the Hindoo God Agni, or Fire, is very important. Zoroaster, in the Zend-Avesta, taught that there was a spirit of Good or Light—Ormuzd, and a spirit of Evil or Darkness—Ahriman, with a number of inferior good and bad genii.

The majority of the inhabitants of India practise a religion known as Brahminism or Hindooism, which, like allied creeds, teaches the mystical absorption of everything in the One, or Deity, and the lack of worth of the human personality. Brahma is the ruler of the universe, Vishnu is the preserver, and Siva the destroyer. Vishnu, according to the Indian sacred chronicles (Vedas and Shastres), is to interfere ten times to deliver the world before it is destroyed. He has already delivered it nine times, and each of these times is known as an incarnation or avatar, or an appearance upon earth of this deity, who usually comes in the form of an animal. Doorga, or Kalee, is the female partner of Siva, and she is supposed to wear two dead bodies as earrings, a necklace of skulls, and the hands of several slaughtered giants circling her waist. Some have reckoned as many as 330, 000, 000 of minor deities in India. Everything almost is worshipped; and it is characteristic of the devotees to regard entire inaction as the most perfect state, and to describe the Supreme Being as "The Unmovable." The river Ganges is a great object of devotion. Into this sacred water, which proceeds through all parts of India, the people crowd to bathe; and until recently they swore by the Ganges (as we do by the Bible) in the courts of law. All sorts of animals are deified, and hospitals are erected for affording shelter and succour to sick and infirm brutes, including lice, fleas, and other vermin. A particular class of devotees, called Fakirs, endure the severest tortures. Bishop Heber mentions a case of one hopping about upon one foot having made a vow never to put the other, which was now contracted and useless, to the ground. It is only in recent years that the British Government has put a stop to such religious practices as the throwing of children into the Ganges, the burning of old women, the *suttee* or custom of a widow cremating herself on the funeral pile of her husband, and the festival of Juggernaut, which was an idol-car dragged along, its path being marked by the bodies of mangled victims, who voluntarily threw themselves before the wheels to be crushed to death.

Buddhism, the religion of Buddh, prevails in Burmah, China, and such districts, and is the most prevalent form of religion upon earth, some 400 million people following it. It is curious in this connection that the Chinese Government once threatened a certain god with deposition if he should fail to fulfil the prayers of the people.[1]

It is the purest form of paganism, has only one idol, and is distinguished by the peculiarity that it lacks any existing god. Adoration is paid to the image of Bood, or Gautama, who was a god at a former period, having lived through 400 millions of worlds, and in every sort of shape and form. The Dzat and Bedagat are the sacred books of this superstition, and the legends contained in them are a fruitful source of designs for Burmah paintings and carvings, which can be seen in the London bazaars or arcades any day. The Buddh who is now worshipped became "nic-banned," or annihilated, over 2,000 years ago; and the next Buddh is to appear in about 7,000 years from the present time. Lamaism is a branch of Buddhism observed in Central Asia and some parts of Russia. When the Grand Lama expires one of his priests, who conveniently becomes inspired, succeeds him. Pilgrimages are paid to worship the Grand Lama in the flesh, and he sometimes distributes as charms gilt balls of consecrated dough, which the Tartars use in many superstitious practices, otherwise described as pellets made from his excrement.

"There is no god but God, and Mohammed is his prophet," is the creed of those who profess Mohammedanism—or, to speak more correctly, Islamism. Islam means submission to the will of God, and every man who makes this profession in Arabia, Egypt, Africa, and the Moorish States is a Moslem or Mussulman. Islamism was the first pagan religion which professed a pure theism, or belief in one God; and, as it was improved under Mohammed beyond the ancient Arabian original from which he took it, the creed has flourished so successfully as to boast at present over 100,000,000 believers. Mohammed was born in Mecca in A.D. 569. After some years spent in commercial pursuits, he conceived the idea of replanting the religion of Christianity. He circulated the story that the angel Gabriel one night came to him, opened his breast, took out his heart, and, after washing it in a golden basin full of water of faith, restored it to its place. He was then brought through seven heavens made of gold, silver, etc., until he arrived at the Heaven of Light, where God from his throne delivered him the Koran for a new divine law. Collecting some disciples, Mohammed aroused antagonism in those who worshipped the old idols, and he was driven from Mecca in A.D. 622. This expulsion is called the Hegira. At Medina, Mohammed collected an army, and, after much fighting, he conquered Arabia and established his religion. And ten years after Hegira he died, no one knowing where he was buried, leaving a daughter, Fatima. The Koran consists of 114 chapters, made up from the Bible and Eastern superstitions, and inculcates that Mohammed succeeded Jesus as the prophet of God. Each Mohammedan must pray three times a day, with his face turned towards Mecca, and perform a pilgrimage to Mecca once in his life, unless prevented by poverty or ill health. The green crescent (green turbans are always worn by aristocratic Mohammedans) is the Phallic symbol of Mohammedanism, as the cross is that of Christianity.

The records of the legendary knowledge of the Scandinavians are the *Eddas* and *Sagas* of Iceland. In these we learn the Northern notions about heroes, deities, the creation of the world, and prophetic revelation. Like the ancient Greeks, the Scandinavians had seats of the blessed and of the gods, which they called Asgard and Valhalla. The great warriors were made gods, and were ruled over by Odin, the chief deity. The Northmen believed that the world originally was a mass of vapours, peopled by a race of evil spirits. Odin slew one of these, and made the world out of his corpse. The great hall where the blessed went was Valhalla; and the pleasures of this palace were the company, the hacking of each other to pieces, and drunken feasts, where enemies' skulls were used for goblets. From some of the gods of these people we have derived many of our words, such as Thursday (Thors-day), Wednesday (Odin's-day), etc.; and in remote and ignorant parts of Shetland and Orkney many Scandinavian superstitions still survive.

Our own ancestors worshipped this Scandinavian deity (Odin), as well as idols emblematic of sun, moon, earth, and seasons. They tattooed themselves; they knocked out their front teeth in sign of mourning; they wore their own hair long, and shaved their wives—a mark of slavery; they took a bride by force; they believed themselves to be descended from a wild animal of some kind, and worshipped those totems of their kindred who still clung to fur or feathers. Sometimes they claimed lineage with a tree or a stone. They sacrificed to a goddess called Eostre, the Easter of the Christians. On that day in December when the days began to lengthen a log of wood was devoutly burned as a Phallic emblem of returning light and heat. This is the origin of our custom of burning the Yule Log. The Druidism of the Ancient Britons gave way to the witchcraft and divination brought in by the Anglo-Saxon. Even in the sixteenth century our predecessors believed profoundly in personal visits of the Devil to our shores.

The scandalous lives of the clergy, the gross reverence paid to relics, the extravagant sale of indulgences, the plundering called tithe, the exhibition of religious things—a skull or bone professing to belong to saints, bits of Christ's cross cut from the neighbouring tree, the spear and cross of the crucifixion, the *veronica* or reputed portrait of the agonising Saviour impressed on the napkin with which the attendant wiped the death sweat from his face, the clothes and manger of Christ, the vessels in which he converted water into wine at the marriage feast, the bread which he broke at the last supper, portions of the burning bush and of the manna which fell in the wilderness, of Moses' rod and Samson's honeycomb, of Tobit's fish, of the Virgin's milk, and of St. Januarius's and our Saviour's blood, are all contemporary features of the popular faith, which have their counterparts in the grossest paganism.

The lingering survivals of legend interpreted as inspired fact are also the staple of sacred systems. Apart from orthodoxy, religion is assuming a "revealed," "inspirational," or "psychical" form, which suggests a recurrence to barbaric times. No better type of this "departure" can be quoted than the "Scientific Religion" evolved by the late Mr. Laurence Oliphant. This gentleman gave his spiritual allegiance to Mr. Harris, the apostle of the semi-Swedenborgian doctrine of "Open or Divine Respiration." In his "Sympneumata" he announces the need of a perfect union between the *pneuma* or spirit of the unseen and the natural man. "Sin" is simply the influence of the living mind being infested with the spirits of the wicked dead. God is bisexual, or our infinite mother as well as our infinite father, and Christ is embodied in the divine feminine. There is a "dynaspheric force" through which we can communicate with the deities; and, by comporting ourselves *a la* Madame Blavatsky, we may attain perfection. These notions fairly sample a not uncommon sort of mind—a mind whose emotional needs require it to compromise with conscience and imagine powers behind.

It may be granted that Christianity, as it is in *spirit*, is holding its own. Though the popular theologies are still saturated with such superstitions as the belief in the objective efficacy of sacerdotal supplications, humiliations, and asceticisms, supernatural revelations, and exclusive salvations, the expansion of science must eventually explode them. The broad principles of Messianic morality underlie in some form the many religions of the world; and there are few, if any, peoples who have no well-defined belief in Deity or a future state of existence. The enumeration of the inhabitants in the known world in regard to religion is authoritatively given thus: —

- Christian Religion — 370, 000, 000
- Jewish — 8, 000, 000
- Pagan — 862,000,000
- Uncivilised — 196,600,000

In England alone there are over 180 certified religions, and every year records schisms. The cause of this sectionising springs, on the one hand, from a growing and *positive* unbelief; and, on the other, from a conscientious revolt against the dogma and formalism of Christianity as it is mistaught by half-lettered traders in the gospel. A peculiar illustration of the commercial side of Christianity is the movement in Japan to make it the State religion, instead of the old Buddhist faith. The motive of this is alleged to be political, for the Japanese declare that the European nations will not treat with them on fair terms unless they embrace Bible beliefs, to which they object, because (according to Max Muller) Christianity makes "dangerous subjects." The worst enemies of orthodoxy are the orthodox themselves. Weekly we find the high priests of Bible worship almost without the professional aside, the *salva reverentia* of custom, impugning the veracity of their own oracle. Christianity is apologised for, and, as its votaries do not like to be accused of sun-worship or Sabaistic heresies, the Druidical mistletoe sinks to the level of "kiss in the ring," the Pyramids serve as a means of support to rascally Arabs, and the cromlechs, instead of Phallic relics, are a convenience for uneasy cattle.

According to Dean Ramsay, 4,000,000 sermons are preached every year in Great Britain. These 4,000,000 sermons are listened to by only 30 per cent, of our population, while 70 per cent, can do without them. The 100 per cent., however, have to pay annually £10,211,321 (exclusive of payments made by Roman Catholics and Jews). Assuming that each sermon takes up only thirty minutes, we arrive at a period of 83,333 days, or about 229 years, half of which at least is annually spent by the combined efforts of the clergy in discussing dogmatic matters. As to material, if every sermon were only fifteen pages in length, the amount spoken annually would furnish us with 60,000,000 pages, or 83,333 volumes of 720 pages each. How much of this collective brain force and complex lung power has been used to bring about a union between Christ's enactments and our diametrically-opposed social organisation?

The problem of the time hence takes this form: What is *vital* religion? Is it something, as Spencer alleges, concerned with what lies beyond the sphere of sense; a consciousness of inscrutable power beyond phenomena, intuition, and imagination; a sentiment suggested by the primitive belief in ghosts, accompanied by a strong fear and worship of the supernatural? Is it nothing but legendary transition from ancestor-worship to the pantheon of the pagan deities, from this to the awe-inspiring Jahveh of the Hebrews and the eclectic ethics of the Christian God of Love? Is it a mere metaphysical disease, or an ideal which incorporates tolerable commonplace virtues and feelings such as love, awe, sympathy, reverence, goodness, life, and creative energy—a mere anthropic deity of qualities? Or is it the attempt to solve Carlyle's problem of a spiritual life neither self-imprisoned in a system nor in bondage to outward form and ceremony? Is it but one form of sensualism, designed to provoke joyful animal spirits and stimulate the functional and emotional natures? May it not be, as Henrik Ibsen preaches, that the development of society is checked by its own hypocrisy, and that salvation lies the way of freedom in the spiritual growth of each individual? Can we, as Dr. Martineau examines in his "Ideal Substitutes," find any proper deputy for God? What is the new theosophy to be— what the deepest speculative wisdom of a scientific age? Will it centre round spirit or sense, or spirit in sense, as Rossetti believed? Will men accept the consolation of Voltaire, that where you have not a god you must create one, and compromise with fate in placing terrors where nothing is known? Will they penetrate the Inscrutable and unveil the truly magical and mysterious?

---

1. Confucianism and Taoism, with their sacred books of Kings and Tao-te-King, are the religions of the Chinese.

Copyright © 2021 by FV Éditions
Illustrations : Publicdomainreview.org (*J. Van de Velde, A. Kircher, Flamsteed*)
Ebook ISBN : 979-10-299-1214-6
Paperback ISBN : 979-10-299-1215-3
Hardcover ISBN : 979-10-299-1216-0
All rights reserved.

Also Available

www.ingramcontent.com/pod-product-compliance
Lightning Source LLC
LaVergne TN
LVHW041850070526
838199LV00045BB/1534